THE LAND
OF
PROMISE

THE LAND
OF
PROMISE

Claiming Your
Christian Inheritance

A.B. SIMPSON

CHRISTIAN PUBLICATIONS

CAMP HILL, PENNSYLVANIA

Christian Publications
3825 Hartzdale Dr, Camp Hill, PA 17011

Faithful, biblical publishing since 1883

ISBN: 0-87509-621-2
LOC Catalog Card Number: 95-70300
© 1996 by Christian Publications
All rights reserved
Printed in the United States of America

96 97 98 99 00   5 4 3 2 1

Cover photo by
Patricia Scrignoli, Positive Images

CONTENTS

CHAPTER 1

Looking Over

Then Moses climbed Mount Nebo from the plains of Moab to the top of Pisgah, across from Jericho. There the LORD showed him the whole land—from Gilead to Dan, all of Naphtali, the territory of Ephraim and Manasseh, all the land of Judah as far as the western sea, the Negev and the whole region from the Valley of Jericho, the City of Palms, as far as Zoar. Then the LORD said to him, "This is the land I promised on oath to Abraham, Isaac and Jacob when I said, 'I will give it to your descendants.' I have let you see it with your eyes, but you will not cross over into it." (Deuteronomy 34:1-4)

When God took Moses up into the top of Pisgah He showed him all the land of Palestine. There are few scenes on earth that could afford such a prospect as was spread out before him there. There are few such views of natural beauty and grandeur as that which can be seen from the heights of Moab, from the sides of Olivet or from the mountains of Lebanon. The picture is exquisitely beautiful in itself. But there is an added charm to it from its historical associations. There is a sacred meaning connected with every scene which one would think must appeal even to the heart that cares little for heavenly things.

It is not our intention now, however, to look at the land topographically, historically or geographically. Rather we want to find in it a symbol of one great inheritance in Christ—a special type of what God would have us see in Him, and enter upon as our own spiritual possession.

Moses had now led the hosts of Israel for 40 years. He had shared in all their trials and had led them to the borders of the inheritance promised to their fathers; but now at the last, by an act of unbelief, he had forfeited the right to enter it with them. This scene upon which he was looking now was the last view God gave him of the land which he could not enter. From the top of Pisgah God gave him a view of the glorious inheritance that others were to enter upon. There is given still to the soul, a revelation, by the Spirit of God, of every experience before it becomes real. We see Christ as a Savior before we take Him to be ours. So also is it with the deeper experiences of His grace.

Moses was only allowed to look over into this possession from the heights of Nebo. God is calling us not only to look upon it, but to enter into it and enjoy it.

A Supernatural Vision

It was a supernatural vision. No one could have

shown it to him but God. " 'No mind has con-
ceived what God has prepared for those who love
him.' but God has revealed it to us by his Spirit"
(1 Corinthians 2:9-10). "The man without the
Spirit does not accept the things that come from
the Spirit of God, for they are foolishness to him,
and he cannot understand them, because they are
spiritually discerned" (2:14).

The most intellectual and cultured minds often
fail most utterly to comprehend the simple gospel
of redemption. They cannot understand the
atonement of Jesus Christ. The mystery of an indwelling Savior, a life of victory over sin and of
rest and peace in God, are beyond their compre-
hension. If you talk to them of a constantly victorious Christian life, it seems to them like foolish
sentimentalism.

From their high, intellectual standpoint they
look down with a kind of pity upon the morbid
fancies of an emotional religion. They have no
sympathy with the idiosyncrasies of the people
who profess such things. They consider them an
uncultured class who are living on the lower plane
of their emotional nature. Yet often such people
have been changed by the power of the Holy
Spirit. Through the pressures of some heavy trial,
or by means of a personal revelation, God had
shown to them a new world of blissful reality in
Himself. He sets their feet all at once on Pisgah's
heights and what before had seemed to be the
meaningless and insignificant, suddenly becomes
tangible and sublime. What they had considered

as the toys of a child, now take their true place above the higher conceptions of genius. God has brought them to the land of promise, and He only could have done it. The Holy Spirit has begun to reveal to them the things of Christ. "The Spirit searches all things, even the deep things of God" (2:10). So the Spirit has shown them the land. They perhaps could not tell how, but somehow He has done it.

Thus God brought Moses to the top of Nebo and somehow gave him a view of all the land. He had taken all the clouds out of the sky and left it clear and transparent. He gave to the eagle eye of His servant, not yet dimmed by age, supernatural strength to take in the glorious vista spread out before him. His eye took in all the details of the picture, from the snowy summits of Lebanon down to the southern limits of the land, and from the sparkling waters of the Mediterranean to the palm trees nestling around the city of Jericho at his feet. It was all one exquisite picture of loveliness.

I believe Moses not only took it in topographically, but that he saw, too, the spiritual meaning of it all, as it was afterwards unfolded in the teachings of the Scriptures. I believe his mind was illuminated by the Holy Spirit to see in this land a type of experience of the Church in the ages to follow.

Have you so seen it, friend? Perhaps you have not become simple and humble enough for it, as teachable as a little child. "If any one of you thinks he is wise by the standards of this age, he should

become a 'fool' so that he may become wise"
(3:18). "As it is written: 'He catches the wise in
their craftiness' " (3:19). You cannot see the land
with your heads; the view must come from the
heart. The apostle prayed for the Ephesian church
that their hearts might be enlightened to know the
riches of the glory of their inheritance (Ephesians
1:18).

There are many intellectual Christians who do
not see all that God has for them in this life. The
Church needs to get her eyes opened to see the
land. She may admit there is much yet unattained,
but she has not seen it. Ask the Lord to show you
your full redemption rights in Christ. Ask Him to
show you the unappropriated promises of your
Bible. Only He can give you the vision of your
substance. And He is ready to anoint your eyes
with eye-salve that you may see.

Like Moses, many do not see the land until they
are about to die. Like him they wander about all
their days, and at last, near the close of life, they
catch a glimpse of what they might have had all
the time, but which they cannot now enter upon.
They must leave the picture for others. All they
can see before them is the banks of Jordan. They
cannot cross them and enter the fields beyond.
They will be with Christ in heaven, and will see
Him at His coming, but they have missed forever
what might have been theirs in their earthly life.

However much we may admire the character of
Moses and reverence his memory, we must not
forget that he lost something. He gained many

crowns, but he did not gain the land of promise. I believe many Christians realize on their deathbed what they have lost. If they had known earlier what they find out then, theirs would have been lives of more constant joy, victory and usefulness; but it is too late. They are saved, but they have lost much out of life that God would have given them.

It is possible for you to see too late what God had for you in this life. It is a blessed thing to know about it, and to tell Joshua to enter in. It is more blessed for you yourself to enter in. God help you not to disappoint yourself or Him! May you not have too late a vision of a life that has ended in disappointment instead of triumph! May your soul perceive the vision of the end, and enter at once upon the possession of all the fullness of Jesus!

In order to see the land of promise you must get above the level of the natural world. You cannot see it while you are wandering on the plains below. You must get to the top of Pisgah to behold it. You must get on higher ground, the ground of consecration. You must be above the world, with your back to its allurements. Everything else must be counted vain and worthless beside the privilege of that glorious view. Lift up your eyes to the place of separation, then go up there alone like Moses. He did not see it in a prayer meeting or amid the noise of thousands. He was alone with God. With Him he climbed the steps up that dizzy height. It was a difficult and solitary way, but it was necessary for God to get him apart from human counsels, and in the silence of that lonely mountain to speak to him face to face. Moses did not fear that all-penetrating light upon his heart of hearts. Have you thought what it must be to be absolutely alone in His presence? It was a blessed place to Moses. All heaven was open to him there with all its possibilities of blessing.

You Must Die

To get a view of the land of promise you must get to the place of death. You must go up that mountainside to die. Moses knew he would never come down from Pisgah. He saw his own sepulcher first, then he saw the land. He did not go up there to become glorified or exalted in himself. It was death to his own pride and goodness and wisdom. When he saw his lonely grave in Moab's land, then God could show him all the land.

When we get there, God can not only show us the land, but bring us in, something He didn't do for Moses. The veil of the flesh is in the way of the Holy of Holies. It must be rent by crucifixion to self. The glory must be opened up to us as it was to Jesus on Calvary. We must die, like Moses, to our own self-will, our glory, our pride, our sensitiveness, the affections that are not utterly of God and for God, our gratifications, our personal aims, our very fear of dying. Perhaps you are afraid of missing something when you are thus dead; well, go to Him and die to that fear. No harm can come to you if you are in the hand of your Father and Savior.

I do not know that we can actually die, but we can be willing to die. Moses did not fear when God took his hand and laid him in the grave. I am glad we do not have to crush this evil thing and tear out that sin. I am glad we have only to go to Nebo's top and look up into the face of love, and then pass away upon His bosom. We will awake and find the old life gone and henceforth Christ living in us.

God has buried the old will and strength, and we do not know what has become of it. We have gone out of self, and we have no consciousness but of God. He has separated us unto Himself. The apostle says it is possible for us to be in this place. "If by the Spirit you put to death the misdeeds of the body, you will live" (Romans 8:13). Are you willing to go there and have the sentence of death pronounced upon you? It is a solemn hour in the lives of many. It seems as if you must actually die. There are things that you hold almost dearer than life that must go out forever. It will be an unutterable surprise to you, when the surrender is really made, to find out that nothing is lost after all.

When Isaac lay upon the altar, it must have seemed to Abraham that all was lost. The bitterness of death was past when God spoke, "Do not lay a hand on the boy" (Genesis 22:12). The inner life of self, the strong will of both Abraham and Isaac died in that hour. When all is yielded to God, absolutely and unconditionally, come what may, there is no place so safe or so sweet as the altar of Moriah, the grave of Nebo, the sepulcher of Jesus.

The Deeper Spiritual Meaning

Not only did Moses behold the land of promise with his outward eyes, but he saw its deeper, spiritual meaning as perhaps no other of the ancient prophets. In his ministry and in his writings, Moses revealed the deeper and higher experiences and truths of which Canaan was a type. They are all one great object lesson revealing the land of promise. Who is the grandest type of faith in all the world? Who was told to turn his back on his kindred and his land, and to step out in the darkness upon the bare promises of God? Abraham. And who gave us the character of Abraham? Moses. Moses also gave us that other picture of the death of self that we must pass through before entering Canaan—Jacob. He was the crookedest and most perverse of God's children, until slain by the hand of God at Peniel. After that he went forth as a prince having power to prevail with God and men. Moses, too, gave us that redemption picture of the blood of the Paschal lamb, the sacrifices on the brazen altar and all the continuous portraiture of Jesus displayed in the tabernacle services.

What is it all but Moses viewing the land and showing it to us? Jesus Himself said, "Moses . . . wrote about me" (John 5:46). From the top of Pisgah he saw the luxuriant fields and forests of Bashan. Then his eye swept past orchards and meadows to the snow-crowned peaks of Lebanon, or followed the silver line of Jordan down to where the Sea of Galilee lay among the hills like a diamond set in emeralds. From Hermon his eye glanced over to the bosom of the Mediterranean, then down the broad lands of Ephraim and Manasseh, and to the hills of Judah and Jerusalem. Perhaps it rested last upon a little hill outside of Jerusalem, where in vision he may have seen a cross erected and One upon it in the agony of death. Perhaps the Spirit whispered to him that was the meaning of the Paschal lamb, and the brazen altar and the tabernacle of Israel.

Then as his eye rested for a moment upon the white peaks of Hermon, He may have beheld another scene in which he himself should take part, as the heavens opened, and the transfiguration glory descended upon the Son of Man, even Him who was to come as the fulfillment of the law and the prophets, Jesus himself, the Son of God, who afterwards came to fulfill the vision He had given to Moses. He revealed Himself to Moses no doubt as the significance of all he saw. He would not show the land to him apart from His own coming and His redeeming work. Moses must have seen Jesus through all his own types as the end of the law and the substance of all truth and life.

The Deeper Truths

The teachings of Moses unfold the deeper truths of the spiritual life. The cleansing of the leper speaks to us of cleansing from the deep poison of sin, which has gone through all our nature. The ordinance of the red heifer teaches the need of keeping the soul from the touch of death and a defiling world.

The feasts of Moses point also to Jesus and His finished work. The Passover speaks of redemption; the feast of Pentecost, of the outpouring of the Holy Spirit; the feast of Tabernacles, of the glorious fruition of His whole redemption, when He will come in the glory of His Father and all the holy angels with Him to sit upon His millennial throne. All this was pictured in the annual feasts.

Nowhere do we find rest more beautifully typified than in the sabbatic feasts. The weekly sabbath, the sabbatic year coming every seventh year, the year of Jubilee every 50th year, all speak of rest in God. The whole Mosaic system teaches the closest communion with God. The tabernacle itself is the very picture of a sanctified life more full and deep than the highest Christian experience has ever fathomed.

Probably Moses knew much of this, and in the vision of the land he saw in vision all he had taught in symbol. We too will understand the meaning of the land of promise as we stand with him and look over its broad fields in the light of the later Scriptures and in that of the Holy Spirit.

Not only does Moses unveil it, but all the Scriptures are full of the vision. David wrote of this land in the Psalms, "Blessed are those who have learned to acclaim you, who walk in the light of

your presence, O Lord. They rejoice in your
name all day long; they exult in your righteousness" (Psalm 89:15-16). "Blessed are those you
choose and bring near to live in your courts! We
are filled with the good things of your house, of
your holy temple" (65:4). "They feast on the
abundance of your house; you give them drink
from your river of delights" (36:8).

Isaiah saw a vision of the ransomed coming to
Zion with songs and everlasting joy upon their
heads. "And a highway will be there; it will be
called the Way of Holiness. The unclean will not
journey on it; it will be for those who walk in that
Way; wicked fools will not go about on it. No lion
will be there, nor will any ferocious beast get up
on it; they will not be found there. But only the
redeemed will walk there" (Isaiah 35:8-9).

As he looked over the land, he saw it bathed in
the very sunlight of heaven, and radiant as with
the very joy of the Marriage Feast. "Your sun will
never set again, and your moon will wane no
more; the Lord will be your everlasting light, and
your days of sorrow will end" (60:20). "No longer
will they call you Deserted, or name your land
Desolate. But you will be called Hephzibah, and
your land Beulah; for the Lord will take delight in
you, and your land will be married" (62:4).

Joel, Micah, Habakkuk, Zechariah, indeed all
the ancient prophets wrote of this glorious land.

How has Jesus painted it? "Come to me, all you
who are weary and burdened, and I will give you
rest. Take my yoke upon you and learn from me,

for I am gentle and humble in heart, and you will find rest for your souls" (Matthew 11:28-29). "I have told you these things, so that in me you may have peace. In this world you will have trouble. But take heart! I have overcome the world" (John 16:33).

Paul speaks of the land of promise in this way. "So that Christ may dwell in your hearts through faith. And I pray that you, being rooted and established in love, may have power, together with all the saints, to grasp how wide and long and high and deep is the love of Christ, and to know this love that surpasses knowledge—that you may be filled to the measure of all the fullness of God" (Ephesians 3:17-19).

John lived in the land. "There is no fear in love. But perfect love drives out fear, because fear has to do with punishment. . . . We love because he first loved us" (1 John 4:18-19). "No one who lives in him keeps on sinning" (3:6). "We know that anyone born of God does not continue to sin; the one who was born of God keeps him safe, and the evil one cannot harm him" (5:18).

So we might go up to the top of many a Pisgah and see what the departing saints saw as they passed away. The martyrs of the primitive ages, the Christian heroes of the past, the sainted ones of all time, found this land real.

> I cannot tell the art
> By which such bliss is given;
> I know thou hast the heart,
> And I have heaven.

Let us get up into the mountain and look over, and then enter upon it. I am glad that it is not a faraway land. Its borders are close beside us. One step into the stream, and we are there.

Let us sum up the landscape in conclusion. First, in that land there is reality. It is not all promise and hope and make believe. There is reality in faith. Jesus becomes a real Sanctifier and a lasting sanctification.

Second, it is a land of rest, not only from care and fret and trouble, but rest in the living God. It is the peace of God that surpasses all understanding. There is something imparted to the soul that is full of rest. There is a calm upon the heart, as though a heavenly hand had been laid upon it and had stilled all its flutterings. The peace of Jesus has taken the place of fears and distractions. It is supernatural calm. One almost wonders how in the midst of things that are enough to drive one crazy, the soul can be kept in peace, like the very breath of heaven. This is what the land has for you. You can always find it in Christ. He wants to put it into your breast. Have you entered into His rest?

A Land of Victory

Next, it is a land of victory. You are not to be beaten and baffled always in your life, but to overcome sin and Satan. You are to be triumphant in the hard places, to be master of the difficulties and trials, pushing through the obstacles and accomplishing your work for God in spite of them. That is the land of promise. We have not enlisted for a battle, but for a campaign. He who has led you through a hundred battles will lead you through a hundred more. It is a hard fight, but it is glorious. Have you this line of victory, my friend? Are you being beaten, or are you overcoming? The battle is not too hard. Say as Caleb did, "The LORD helping me, I will drive them out" (Joshua 14:12).

Take care lest you think the difficulties cannot be overcome. Take care how you fail to go forward to meet them in Christ. There is a life of victory for you even if you are not in it; but do not stop until you have it in all its fullness.

Then, there is not only deliverance from guilt, but there is real holiness in the land. God wants and means to have all the beauty and grace of Jesus Christ put into your life and wrought out in your character. What would the land be without the grapes of Eshcol?

What are the fruits of this land? Paul speaks of them in the epistle to the Galatians, "But the fruit of the Spirit is love, joy, peace, patience, kindness, goodness, faithfulness, gentleness and self-control" (Galatians 5:22-23). These are the grapes of Eshcol. They do not grow out of you, but out of the land. You cannot make them. Get the heavenly vine and they will be on it. If you are a part of the vine they cannot help growing upon you.

Next, the inheritances in that land are not confused and jumbled together, so that every one shares alike. Each has his own inheritance. They had theirs in the literal Canaan, and it is true also of the spiritual land. Each of us can have the best thing possible for us in the will of God. He will give to us just what will yield us the greatest, real blessing, and which will in every way make the most of us.

God has a place for you as a bookkeeper, a carpenter, a missionary, or a humble shepherd of the flock. Have you got all there is in life for you? Have you missed nothing? Have you taken into this short life all God would press into it? Can you say as Joshua did: "Not one of all the LORD's good promises to the house of Israel failed" (Joshua 21:45). It would be a terrible thing to miss what He made and redeemed you for. Your soul may not be lost, but there will have gone out of your life beautiful, precious things like clusters of radiant gems. God help you to take them and make them your own.

Then, there is power and blessing for others in the land through your ministry. Your life will tell for good to them. It will never thus tell until you have risen in a higher level to your own experience.

Last, the land was not far away from the mountain where Moses stood; it was lying at his feet. A few days after, the children of Israel entered upon it. Do not say that it is at such a distance and will take a long time to reach it. The land is very near. What did Caleb say? "We should go up and take possession of the land, for we can certainly do it" (Numbers 13:30). They were willing to go some time afterward, but God was not. They tried to go

on the morrow, but God would not go with them.
Before this chapter closes your feet may have
taken the first step of full commitment. Before tomorrow morning you may have fought a hundred
battles and overcome in all. May the Lord say to
you today, "Go up at once and possess it."

How sad that Moses saw the land but could not
enter it. He was a good man, yet he yielded for a
moment to doubt and haste, and lost a great blessing. There are people of God today who are missing much of the precious things they might
receive. I am glad Moses was under the law, and
we are under the gospel. Moses could not enter in
because he represented that law. Joshua alone
could go into the land because he represented the
gospel. Jesus has come to lead you in, beloved.

Do not waste time in trying to get there yourself. Christ only can lead you in. Can you say, as
you look over from Pisgah, "We have not received
the spirit of the world but the Spirit who is from
God, that we may understand what God has
freely given to us" (1 Corinthians 2:12). We know
them now. But they are also "freely given to us."
We can have them as a free gift of His infinite
grace. Let us take them and rejoice forever that we
said this hour,

> Lord, I believe a rest remains
> To all Thy people known;
> A rest where pure enjoyment reigns,
> And Thou art loved alone.
> A rest, where all the soul's desire

Is fixed on things above;
Where fear, and sin, and grief expire,
Cast out by perfect love.

Oh! that I now that rest might know,
Believe and enter in;
Now, Saviour, now the gift bestow,
And let me cease from sin.

I rest upon His promise sure,
I come, I wait to prove
The cleansing of my heart from sin,
The fullness of His love.

CHAPTER 2

Setting Out

The LORD had said to Abram, "Leave your country, your people and your father's household and go to the land I will show you." (Genesis 12:1)

The LORD said to Abram after Lot had parted from him, "Lift up your eyes from where you are and look north and south, east and west. All the land that you see I will give to you and your offspring forever. I will make your offspring like the dust of the earth, so that if anyone could count the dust, then your offspring could be counted. Go, walk through the length and breadth of the land, for I am giving it to you." (13:14-17)

The act of setting out for the land of promise is beautifully exemplified in the life of Abraham. At the command of God he left his home in Ur of the Chaldees and emigrated to Palestine, to him, a new and strange land. There are three steps in this pilgrimage which exactly typify the stages of Christian experience at the beginning of a life of entire consecration. First, we see him setting out from the old life and separating from it. Next, we see him coming into the land, believing in it, appropriating it by faith, and taking actual possession of it. Last, we find him walking through the length and breadth of it, and actually entering upon the possession of it day by day in all its fullness.

Separation

Separation was the keynote of Abraham's life, and it is a most important thought in connection with full salvation. We must separate from sin unto holiness, from the old nature unto the new, from the earthly life unto the heavenly. The idea of separation runs all through the history of Abraham.

He was separated from his country. God's call came to him, "Leave your country" (12:1). So, before we can enter the land of promise we must be out of the other land. What is the land God calls us to leave? It is the world. We cannot enter upon the fullness of Christ's salvation and have the pleasures of the world at the same time. The two things cannot go together. The command is as imperative as it was to Abraham. " 'Therefore come out from them and be separate, says the Lord. Touch no unclean thing, and I will receive you.' 'I will be a Father to you, and you will be my sons and daughters, says the Lord Almighty' " (2 Corinthians 6:17-18).

It was not to old Terah that God said this, but to young Abraham. It is not old people, who have taken their fill of pleasure and are tired of it, that God calls to leave their country; but it is to young, fresh hearts, to whom everything is fascinating and delightful, that the word is given. There is great blessing for those who can turn aside from the cup of pleasure, even when it is at their lips and while the ardor of youthful passion is glowing in their hearts. There is no consecration in turning from these things when the taste for them is lost and passion has burned itself out by indulgence.

If we would enter into the land and secure our inheritance there, we must have no aim on earth but to know God and do His will. We must get so stripped of all longings for other things that there will be nothing left of them. Ah! it is blessed to have the heart and will consent unto God in this entire surrender. He does surely fill the soul that is so given up to Him.

Family and Friends

Abraham was called also to leave his people. So we, too, are called to lay on God's altar all the ties of natural affection, all the selfish passions and the loves of earth. His is not the cold and cruel mandate of an unfeeling master. He calls for them that our hearts may be concentrated on Him alone. Then, if they are pure and held only for His glory, He will give them back to us. If they are not so possessed, there will be, there must be, loss.

We must have everything cut off from the earthly side that we may be compensated by a richer growth on the heavenly side. It is a furnace of fire through which the heart must pass. The friendships that are dearer than life cannot be laid down on God's altar without deep anguish, but He is calling for it. If the spouse you count your dearest earthly treasure, or the friend on whose wisdom and affection you depend so implicitly, is hindering God's work in your heart, though it be like taking out your very life, he or she must be laid down. Then, though you can give Him only a broken heart, He will bind it up and fill it with His own holy presence, which will bring a joy and peace utterly unknown before.

His Father's Household

The next call to Abraham was to leave his father's household. I think there is figurative reference in this to use natural descent from our first parents and our relations to the fallen human race. God would have us get out from that life into which we were born. The very nature itself must be left behind. That is where the hardest death comes. The severest strain of all is not to leave your race or your country, or even your human affections, but it is to part with that which is far dearer than them all, your will. You must be separated from the sinful, despotic, old self-life enthroned in the heart.

The instincts of our nature are not to be our guide. We must cease to be directed by them. They can never bring a blessing to those who obey them, whether they are the promptings of self-will, of earthly desire and lust, or what may be termed the highest tastes of refinement and culture. We are not to follow the guidance of human intellect and reason alone, because these things came to us by the creative hand of God, and they have been injured by the fall. Everything that pertains to us naturally is corrupt and fit only for death. God makes no account of them. We must lay all that came to us from the old Adam life upon the block. It must be given up to die that we may be wholly dedicated to the will of God.

Abraham three times suffered this separation from his father's house. Each time the stroke must have been a severe one. The first was in Haran, where his aged father died. Then his nephew, almost the only relative that came with him, would not work in harmony with him. Lot's will was corrupt, and so there had to come another separation. We can imagine with what sorrow the old patriarch parted from Lot. But how grand the unselfishness that gave to his meaner nephew the choice of the best land, as he left him! Lot took it, leaving to Abraham the barren hills upon which to feed his flock, while he went to the rich valley of the Jordan, well watered and fertile as the garden of the Lord. Keenly the old man must have felt the selfish ingratitude, yet for the love he bore his nephew, he made the sacrifice. Lot deliberately chose the world, wounding and disappointing a noble nature in doing so. Many a deep trouble it caused Abraham afterward to deliver Lot from the result of his folly.

The trial that must have gone most deeply to his heart, however, came afterward, when he was called upon to separate himself from the child of promise. Isaac had come as a wonderful fulfillment of the faith that had waited 25 years for him, and he had grown to be the center of all his hopes.

God came again and tested his heart more deeply by demanding the sacrifice of Isaac. After the test God could say to Abraham, "Now I know that you fear God, because you have not withheld from me your son, your only son" (Genesis 22:12). Isaac was the very link of Abraham's faith and hope; nevertheless, when called, he became separated again. That which God had given, Abraham learned to hold only for Him. He would not cling to it for himself.

There is a precious lesson in this for us. The things that God gives to us, and that we hold so dear, are not be prized for the joy they add to us. But we are to receive them in Him as a means of increasing our usefulness in His service. The friends that are so dear to our heart, we must not cling to for ourselves; they are to be held only for God. This is perhaps the most necessary lesson to be learned in the Christian life. God would teach it to the very depths of our souls and make it a part of our spiritual life. We must surrender all to Him. We must hold everything subject to His will, and yet not be afraid that he will do something harsh if they are so yielded. Isaac had to be laid on the altar, but he was not lost. He could not be.

This is to be "pure in heart." The word pure simply means unmixed. "Blessed are the pure in heart" (Matthew 5:3, KJV). That is, blessed are the single in heart. "If your eyes are good, your whole body will be full of light. But if your eyes are bad, your whole body will be full of darkness" (6:22-23).

Have you learned all these lessons of separation? Have you heard God calling you to this, and have you yielded without fear? You need not dread the knife that cuts so deeply into all the quivering flesh of the proud self-life. It wounds only to heal. All you give up of your selfishness will be restored to you a thousand-fold in Him.

A Step of Faith

The next step in Abraham's life was that of faith. He had to take as well as leave. He had to exercise faith without clear light. There was no consciousness of God. He had no way by which his pilgrimage could be guided. He did not go by an express train that was engaged to let him off at the right station. He did not have a map of the desert he was to cross, that would show him even when he reached the end of it. He had only the naked word of the Lord, "Leave your country . . . and go to the land I will show you" (Genesis 12:1). There was nothing definite in the promise. The call was clear but nothing else was. God would be with him and show him the way as he needed to know it. That was all.

When God calls us out of our own land to go to the land of promise, the first thing we have to leave is our preconceived notions of what is to be done. We must set our own ideas aside. God is to be the chief object of our faith and hope. Like the disciples on the Mount of Transfiguration, we are able to see no man but Jesus only. Many of you have the way all mapped out. You have heard someone's experience, and want that itinerary for your journey. He will not lead you, my friend, as He has led me. The road will develop as you go on; you cannot even see twenty-four hours ahead.

Sometimes God may keep you waiting, as He did Abraham for 25 years. You will be tempted today and tried tomorrow. What you have to do is to lean constantly on Jesus; there is no life apart from Him. Nothing else is definite or clear. God will show you the way day by day. Learn to lean on Him more than on His promises. That is the lesson that Abraham learned. He saw Him first and the land afterward. He leaned on Him and went out not knowing where he was going. You, too, do not know how He will lead you; but choose Him anyhow. Happy indeed the heart that can sing:

> I have called thee, "Abba, Father"
> I have stayed my heart on Thee;
> Storms may howl, and clouds may gather.
> All must work for good to me.

Can you say this in the midst of deep sorrow? Have you truly got nothing but Him? If you have,

He will show you many things. He will draw you constantly nearer to Him, and lead you constantly farther on your way, explaining much that is dark to you now. This cannot be, however, until you have Him alone in the world. The heart must be centered on Jesus. You must see nothing but Him in the heights above or in the depths below. He must be to you the substance of all blessing. Then you can take everything else as He gives it. Abraham believed, not the word, he "believed God, and it was credited to him as righteousness" (Romans 4:3). Oh, friend, learn to lean on God, to trust the person of God. Later, you can learn to trust His promises. You can cling to God, not merely to His Word, for the thing you want. He loves to have you cling to Him. You, too, may then be called the friend of God.

A distant promise comes after a little. It is easy to believe that now, for he has already believed the Promiser. When Abraham reached Palestine the Lord said to him. "To your offspring I will give this land" (Genesis 12:7). As if to make the meaning of the promise clear to Abraham's mind, it was coupled with another promise—that he should have a son.

Abraham believed both promises, all the more because he had believed God before. It was hard to believe that the land into which he had come, that was then inhabited by the Canaanites, was one day to be his own. He had to leave it almost as soon as he entered it and go down to Egypt for food. It was hard to believe he should have a son, in his old age, to become the head of the redeemed race. He waited for the fulfillment of this for a quarter of a century. God wanted the promise to mean something to him. The more difficult it was, the more it would show His own almighty hand. Abraham had God, and so he had the guarantee of the promise. God could not fail, and so the promise was secure. Oh, the blessedness of thus leaning on God! You can never know the happiness of a deeper and higher life in Christ till you have learned it.

Again, Abraham believed God for the land and for offspring long before he had any evidence of possessing either. He believed not only when he had no sight, but when everything seemed to be pointing directly the other way. Twenty-five years passed before the promise was redeemed; yet Abraham was no more sure of it when his child was born than he had been during the years of waiting. He had been satisfied that God would keep His word, and it had all along been real to his faith. It is an important lesson for all who would enter into the fullness of Christ. Faith must be the basis of a life of consecration to God. We expect him to remove the difficulties. That is not God's plan. He would have us step out in the midst of the opposing elements and trust him. We cannot stand steadily in the hard place of testing unless we are sure beyond a question that He will stand true to His promise. That is what Abraham did.

If you would come to Christ for sanctification, the first step is to dare to believe that He accepts you as fully as you give yourself to Him, and becomes to you all your need. If you saw it all first, you would not have the blessing of faithful Abraham, who believed the promise while yet its fulfillment was unseen. It is the same for other blessings even in temporal things. All that you will dare to stand upon and claim as yours with unswerving faith, you will receive.

Do not say this is not for you, and that it is a higher style of Christian life than you can reach. Be willing to believe and wait. Perhaps He will not keep you waiting an hour.

Abraham believed God and received the rewards of his faith in the possession of that for which he trusted. The apostle said of him in the epistle to the Romans, "Yet he did not waver through unbelief regarding the promise of God, but was strengthened in his faith and gave glory to God, being fully persuaded that God had power to do what he had promised. This is why 'it was credited to him as righteousness' " (Romans 4:20-22).

Abraham so believed God that he counted "things that are not as though they were" (4:17). He allowed Lot to have his choice of the land, and when he, full of his strong self-life, claimed the best, Abraham let him have it. When we believe God, we can let people have many things that really belong to us. If God had them for us, no one can possibly take them from us. So Lot took the rich plain of the Jordan. God had given it all to Abraham, and he knew he could not lose it.

Can you believe God for your reputation enough to let people say what they like about you? Can you be meek and suffer, knowing that God is your vindicator? Can you let failure and difficulties of all kinds come if He sends them? Can you lose means and friends and yet say, "God has promised all to me, and it is right"? Can you let things seem to be taken from you rather than fight to retain them? Do you understand the meaning of this verse, "the one who trusts will never be dismayed" (Isaiah 28:16)? Do you believe God enough to put Isaac upon the altar and be quiet in the time of testing? Did Abraham believe Isaac would die? Not for one minute! He was the seed of the promise, and Abraham knew he would be preserved. He doubtless did not understand God's leading, but this call could not hinder Isaac's being the child of promise.

If we are sure our Isaacs are the children of promise, if God has told us they are ours, we too can lay them fearlessly on His altar. They cannot die, but they must be surrendered. Then we will know that they cannot be lost. Indeed we do not truly believe God until we are sure of this.

And yet, on the other hand, while Abraham would not contend with Lot for the land, he did contend for it with his enemies. When a band of invaders from Chaldea came into the land, claimed Abraham's inheritance, and took Lot prisoner, the old man rose up for the defense of his inheritance. He used the sword for the first time in his life. He went against the invaders with a small band of trained servants, brought back the fugitives and the spoil they had carried away, and reclaimed the land from the touch of the alien.

So we will resist Satan's attack upon our promises. It is not our province to contend with men, especially our brethren, but the attacks of the devil call for a courageous resistance. We should fear no enemy here, for we will be more than conquerors through Him who loved us.

After Lot was separated from Abraham, God gave him a glorious vision of faith and a renewal of the promise. He said to him: "Lift up your eyes from where you are and look north and south, east and west. All the land that you see I will give to you and your offspring forever. . . . Go, walk through the length and breadth of the land, for I am giving it to you" (Genesis 13:14-17).

Abraham's outlook on the land was not like the one given to Moses from the wilderness on the other side of Jordan, from which he saw a land he could not enter upon. Abraham looked upon it from Hebron, or some mountain in the interior of Palestine. It was a vision after he was in the land. Moses looked only in one direction; Abraham looked north, and south, and east, and west. Lot was down in the valley of the Jordan; Abraham was on the barren hilltop, and his view was unobstructed. Lot, from his position on the low, alluvial plains, could not see very far; he was sunk so low in his selfishness that he could see only the fertile plain. But the grand old patriarch, away upon the Judean hills, had a magnificent outlook over all the land.

Have you ever stood thus upon the barren heights of some great self-denial and looked down upon your land of promise, away up to the distant north, down to the sunny south, yonder to the sunrise in the east, all the way to the setting sun and heavenly horizon in the west? All is yours; all you can apprehend in the vision of faith is your own. Look as far as you can, for it is all yours. The vision of faith is the prophecy of blessing. If there is nothing revealed to you, there can be no meaning in the land for you. No instincts can be put in you by the Holy Spirit but that which He purposes to fulfill. Let your faith then rise and soar away, and claim all the land that you can discover.

All that you long to be as a Christian, all that you long to do for God, are within the possibilities of faith. Then come still closer, and, with your Bible before you, and your soul open to all the influences of the Spirit, let your whole being receive the baptism of His presence. And, as He opens your understanding to see all His fullness, believe that He has it all for you. Accept for yourself all the promises of His Word, all the desires He awakens within you, all the possibilities of what you may be as a follower of Jesus. All the land you see is given to you. Let faith follow hard upon vision.

It was not enough for Abraham to stand upon the mountaintop and look over the land; he had to go down from the height and walk through the length and breadth of it. So, every moment of life to the very end, we must make the land ours step by step. Every little circumstance of life, every minute detail, is to be but another hold upon the land of promise. It is as long as 24 hours in a day, and as 60 seconds in a minute. It is as broad as our spirit's need, as our temptations and our trials, as our body's pains and infirmities, as the cares of the family, the toils of the kitchen, the labor of the workshop, the transactions upon the street, the business of the office, the religious world in which we live, the social circle in which we mingle, the whole world in which we move. It is as long as life and as broad as human need.

Do not say this life cannot be lived in real, practical experience. The best time I know for true consecration is from Monday morning to Saturday night. The hard pull of every day is the best test of the grace of God. Take Jesus this afternoon, this evening, this night. Tomorrow morning begin the day in His presence. Take him for the 50 things that must be thought of perhaps in an hour, so that nothing will be neglected. It is a practical life. Arise and walk through the land, a step at a time. These little steppings alone will make it all your own.

Travelers, who would most thoroughly understand and enjoy the scenery of Switzerland, walk through the valleys and passes of the mountains. Thus only can we know all the fullness of Christ.

> Jesus, my all in all Thou art,
> My rest in toil, mine ease in pain;
> The medicine of my broken heart;

In war, my peace, in loss, my gain;
My smile beneath the tyrant's frown;
In shame, my glory and my crown.

In want, my plentiful supply;
In weakness, mine almighty power;
In bond, my perfect liberty;
My light in Satan's darkest hour;
In grief, my joy unspeakable;
My life in death; my heaven; my all.

CHAPTER 3

Coming Short

When Moses sent them to explore Canaan, he said, "Go up through the Negev and on into the hill country. See what the land is like and whether the people who live there are strong or weak, few or many. What kind of land do they live in? Is it good or bad? What kind of towns do they live in? Are they unwalled or fortified? How is the soil? Is it fertile or poor? Are there trees on it or not? Do your best to bring back some of the fruit of the land." (It was the season for the first ripe grapes.)

So they went up and explored the land from the Desert of Zin as far as Rehob, toward Lebo Hamath. They went up through the Negev and came to Hebron, where Ahiman, Sheshai and Talmai, the descendants of Anak, lived. (Hebron had been built seven years before Zoan in Egypt.) When they reached the Valley of Eschol, they cut off a branch bearing a single cluster of grapes. Two of them carried it on a pole between them, along with some pomegranates and figs. That place was called the Valley of Eschol because of the cluster of grapes the Israelites cut off there. At the end of forty days they returned from exploring the land.

They came back to Moses and Aaron and the whole Israelite community at Kadesh in the Desert of Paran. There they reported to them and to the whole assembly and showed them the fruit of the land. . . .

But the men who had gone up with him said, "We can't attack those people; they are stronger than we are." And they spread among the Israelites a bad report about the land they had explored. They said, "The land we explored devours those living in it. All the people we saw there are of great size." (Numbers 13:17-26; 31, 32)

Let us, therefore, make every effort to enter that rest, so that no one will fall by following their example of disobedience. (Hebrews 4:11)

This is the most vivid and mournful picture of the children of Israel halting on the borders of the promised land.

What spiritual lessons can we learn from this story of their failure? May we not discover in it some of the causes that are keeping many back from entering into the land? There were four general causes for Israel's failure, and they will be found to correspond very closely to the causes of spiritual failure in the church of today.

Human Wisdom

The first of these is dependence on human wisdom. The very appointment of the spies implies a

leaning upon the counsels of man rather than taking the word of God. It is singular that the names
of these men are strongly suggestive of human
wisdom and confidence.

The first was Shammua, the son of Zaccur. The
word Shammua means fame, and Zaccur stands
for distinction. They both suggest human wisdom
and are typical of those things that would lead us
to put confidence in the opinions and traditions of
men. They were leaders who seemed likely to give
wise and good counsel, but they kept Israel from
their inheritance. The preponderance of the brain
over the heart and the simplicity of faith are the
great hindrances to spiritual life. Brilliant qualities
may give intellectual power, but they can never
bring us to the teachings of the Holy Spirit or to
the feet of Jesus, and therefore they stand in the
way of spiritual progress.

There are such leaders as Shammua, the son of
Zaccur, in the world still. They lead their followers into the realms of culture and earthly distinction, but never into the life of faith, or the land of
promise. A highly cultured intellect, though it is
God's gift, is not meant to be the guide of His
people until it has been consecrated at His feet
and filled with the Holy Spirit.

There is no lack of intellectual power in the
leaders of Christianity at the present time, but
they only keep back the children of God from
their true place. Christ was constantly meeting
Shammua, the son of Zaccur, in His ministry. He
warned the people against the teachings of the

rabbis and Pharisees, who could not lead them into the land of rest. Paul had to contend against the wisdom of the Jews and the philosophy of the Greeks. It is the light of God we need, not the conceit of man. "If any one of you thinks he is wise by the standards of this age, he should become a 'fool' so that he may become wise" (1 Corinthians 3:18).

The next leader was Shaphat, whose name means judge. He was a man of strong common sense and sound judgment. It is just as bad to rely upon our own judgment as to lean upon the wisdom of other people.

Joshua was another leader. His name meant Jehovah, my Savior. He represents the spirit of faith and the leadership of Jesus.

We have not time to examine all these names. One other only will we look at. Ammiel means "My people are strong." This man did not trust in wisdom, but in numbers and strength. Does not Christianity sometimes look at its vast machinery, its splendid forces, the strength of its missionary bands and other associations, and say, "My people are strong and great"? Indeed, they are strong collectively. They have force enough to go up and take the world for Christ. They have talented men and gifted women in abundance. The people are strong. But that is not the way to take the kingdom. "Do not be afraid, little flock, for your Father has been pleased to give you the kingdom" (Luke 12:32). The confidence in our strength is always an obstacle to real advancement. It will stand in the way of dependence, and whatever keeps us from getting at the feet of Jesus must be a hindrance.

The very thought of sending the spies was the suggestion of human wisdom. God had said the land was good. Where was the sense in sending to see if it was good? God had told them there were mighty tribes there, but that they should cast them out. What was the use of going to see how strong the Hittites were? God had told them He would be their leader. Why should they try to make a way for themselves?

So man is always doing. He asks God for direction, gets an answer, and then goes and talks to man about it. He receives a message from the Holy Spirit, and immediately begins to question and reason about it, and gets into darkness at once. Be careful of the wisdom of others and of your own reasoning unless both are under the full control of the Spirit of God.

We should be guarded against the traditions and opinions of men. Jesus charged the Pharisees that they made void the Word of God through their traditions. The Apostle Peter tells us that we have been redeemed through the blood of Christ from our vain conversation received by tradition from our fathers.

We need to be guarded also about our own wisdom. We would not discourage careful, deliberate thought before making any important decision in life, nor the seeking of judicious counsel if there is not a certainty in the mind as to the will of God about it. But when His word has been given, when the voice from heaven has spoken clearly, then there should be implicit, unquestioning obedience. There must be a walking alone with God henceforth, and a going forward in His work without fear.

Another thing we need to be guarded against is prejudice. This often gets in the way of God. It induces many Christians to turn away from some of the most precious truths in the Bible, because they have not been taught in that way. Their belief has crystallized into a rigid creed, perhaps much of it human, and there is no moving them. Many are held back from the fullness of perfect liberty in Christ by a set of opinions they have always held, or the doctrine taught in their church, and this deep prejudice is seemingly impossible to uproot. They are prejudiced in favor of certain things and against certain other things. They do not care for a certain class of meetings because it is too sensational or emotional. They will lose their blessing because some heart on fire for God breaks out in praise in the meeting and disturbs their dignity.

The trouble is, although they do not see it, their own prejudices are in the way. It is the head again instead of the heart. Shammua or Shaphat is taking the lead once more. The spies are bringing a false report and are being believed instead of the Holy Spirit.

The one most used of God to bring to me God's message about the deep things of religion was the last person I should have chosen with my head for that purpose. A dear old saint, who knew the Lord better than I, was used to teach me of the indwelling life of Jesus Christ. If I had not been willing to receive the teaching God sent me in that way, I should have lost it. Someone has said, we have to be beheaded first, and then headed up anew before God can bless us. Well, be sure the old head is really cut off. Prejudice, dislike for some person or some set of people, unwillingness to receive the blessing in some way, have kept many of God's children out of the land of blessing for years. We have to come down. Personal prejudice must be given up if we would have fullness of the blessing.

Fear

The next cause of Israel's failure was their fear. Some Christians have always a ready ear when the devil speaks of difficulty. The spies said the land was good, and the grapes were rich and abundant, but the people were mighty. They said the cities were walled up to heaven. Their fears undoubtedly exaggerated also the strength of the enemy. In the eyes of these 10they were giants, and they themselves were like grasshoppers before them. It was all the language of fear.

Job says, "What I feared has come upon me" (Job 3:25). The solemn charge given to Jeremiah was, "Do not be terrified by them, or I will terrify you before them" (Jeremiah 1:17). God looks upon such fear as sin. It is the certain prelude to failure, confusion and disaster. It would be possible to get a complete gospel by stringing together all the

"Fear nots" of God's Word. Oh, friend, be afraid of your fears!

Discouragement and fear on the part of Israel at this crisis sprang from several causes. The chief one was the dwelling upon the greatness of the difficulty itself. It is well to know at the outset that all sorts of difficulties are to be met with in this life. They are there in the path, and they must be overcome, for they are tremendously real. Your home, your associates, your very minister may seem to hinder you in your life of consecration. You must be true, and yet you must keep constantly the sweet spirit of Christ. There are a hundred difficulties that will seem to forbid it. But God is a sufficient power against all these things, whether they come from your disposition and temperament, or from the outward difficulties that meet you in life.

Your body may be weak, and physical infirmity may depress you. But God makes no account of difficulties; take it for granted that they will appear, and do not yield to fear and worry. Stand in His strength. Lay the difficulty over upon Him; He is able to give you the victory. Expect things to be at their worst. If they prove to be easy and delightful, let them come to you as a pleasant surprise. Take hold of His strength expecting you are going to have conflict.

Weakness

The next cause of Israel's failure was looking at their own weakness. Not only did the cities seem too strong to be taken and the men of the land like giants, but they themselves in their own eyes were like grasshoppers. When the soul is ever turned inward upon itself, a great deal can be found that is discouraging. If you look at self, you have no end of trouble. The language of faith will cease. Your difficulties will seem like great cities walled up to heaven, your foes like giants, and you like grasshoppers before them. Even if you are like grasshoppers, what difference does it make anyhow? God is not measuring your strength if He has undertaken to fight your battles for you. He does not expect you to be strong. There are no resources in you at all for the work. Trust in Him and let Him be the victor.

Do not say you have so little talent you have nothing for God, or you cannot speak for Him because you have no ability to influence others. The great majority of people expect God to excuse them from service because they are so small. What God expects of you is victory under all circumstances. It is just as egotistical to think of your weakness as of your strength. All you can possibly bring to God is an empty hand and the spirit of nothingness. He starts in you as the Alpha and He will become the Omega. He is all the real strength you will ever have. He will become faith to you if you will cease from yourself and learn to trust Him.

Take the Holy Spirit as the true gift of wisdom, and He will become in you power for all your Christian service. God wants you to be weak.

"God chose the weak things of the world to shame the strong. He chose the lowly things of this world and the despised things—and the things that are not—to nullify the things that are, so that no one may boast before him" (1 Corinthians 1:27-29).

We can but notice, too, that many are afraid of their reputation and what they may suffer in stepping out too decidedly in Christian life. They are afraid of what people will say, or that the step will cost them some suffering, perhaps the sacrifice of something that is very dear to them if they consecrate themselves fully to God. This one fear stands in the citadel of their will and refuses to surrender. How it makes everything seem black and forbidding that obstructs in any degree the way of this new life. But then, this once given up, the self-life within wholly yielded, the world entirely renounced, how different everything is!

When the Israelites got into the Jordan, they found they were walking through it on dry land. Not a bit of the slime from its bed, or even a drop of its water touched them. It was only a seeming death. There was no real sacrifice after all. So we too find it when we are willing to give up everything to Him. We receive all back from Him, and there is nothing that really amounts to a sacrifice.

All that God wants is a full surrender of the will. Be afraid of your fears, beloved. They will pierce your heart and hinder your advancement. God is calling you forward; the devil is trying to discourage you, and so puts a fear within you.

Dismiss it as an evil thing. The cloud that seems to surround you will turn into the cloud of God's presence, with Jesus in the midst.

Unbelief

Israel failed also because of unbelief. They did not believe God's promises. They did not doubt His power exactly, but they did not set a firm belief in that power over against the difficulty that met them. That is unbelief. You may believe God can do all things, but unless you make that belief of practical use in your hour of trial, you are not really trusting Him. They should have put the power of God over against the Anakim and the walled cities of the plain. Caleb did that. He said, "We should go up and take possession of the land, for we can certainly do it" (Numbers 13:30). They said, "We are not able." When a pressure of trouble comes, it is so easy to look at it and fail to see the help God has for it. They needed to take His power for the difficulty.

David says, "I have set the LORD always before me. Because he is at my right hand, I will not be shaken" (Psalm 16:8). That is faith. Everything else is unbelief. If you really believe God, you will take hold of His omnipotence for every difficulty, whether it is great or trifling. Have you got a bad temper? You will see that God is able to fill it with His sweetness. Have you a strong, dominant will? God is able to make it pliable by His touch. Are the people around you holding you back from the place you long to occupy in Christ? God is able to manage them and make them instruments of blessing in your life. The harder the place, the more He loves to show His power. If you wish to find it real, come to Him in some great trouble. He has no chance to work until you get into a hard place. He led Israel out of the usual way till He got them to the Red Sea. Then there was room for His power to be manifested. God loves the hard places and the narrow places.

Rejoice, if you are in such a place. Even if it is in the very heart of the foe, God is able to deliver you. Let not your faith in Him waver for a moment, and you will find His omnipotence is all upon your side for every difficulty in which you can be placed.

The Israelites also doubted his love. "Why is the LORD bringing us to this land only to let us fall by the sword? Our wives and children will be taken as plunder" (Numbers 14:3). They thought God had brought them there to destroy them, and that He was against them and no longer loved them. Everything seemed to work adversely in their lives. They could give no other reason for it than that God had ceased to be their friend. Can you see in this state any mirror of your mind? Does doubt of His love ever come to you when difficulties increase?

Temptations may attack us like a fierce tempest, but we should be able to believe that God is in the very midst of the whirlwind. You are not going to perish if you will but trust Him. The enemy is always ready to come back with his old serpent's hiss, and whisper in your ear that these troubles have all come because you have done something wrong, and that you are not one of God's chosen ones. By listening to him you are sure to grieve away the Spirit. He presses the barb deeper and deeper into your soul, until he plunges you into the darkness of despair.

How often in the moment of temptation doubt comes into the weakened soul as to whether it is saved, and distrust of God's love is sure to follow! I think it would be better to doubt the power of God even, than His love. Never do that, friend. Though unworthy, believe His love to you without a question. It hinders many from receiving the fullness of His salvation, and it comes because they do not know the heart of God.

He loved us when there was no beauty in us. But He looked ahead and saw what He could make of us in Christ. And so He took us, all unlovely as we were, and is transforming us into the loveliness of Christ. It all comes from the wealth of His grace to us. When the change is completed we will see that through it all God has had nothing in His heart for us but love. It was a revelation of heaven when I dared to believe the promise, "I have sworn not to be angry with you, never to rebuke you again" (Isaiah 54:9). Only as you believe this word can you go forth and take the word of victory.

Doubting God's Word

The Israelites also doubted the word and promise of God. They refused to believe in His truth.

He said He would bring them into the land and
they doubted it. At the very entrance of it they
were thrown into bewilderment and confusion by
the report of the spies. They did not believe that
God would be with them in every step if they entered it. They failed, as too many people do today,
to count God's word a perfect word and already
fulfilled in His sight when it is given to us. It is
not a future thing, but a past one to God.

This is another reason why so many fail to enter into the fullness of Jesus. They want to feel the
help He has for their body or for their life. God
wants them to believe it anyhow, without doubting, no matter what they see. That is what He
calls faith. "See to it, brothers, that none of you
has a sinful, unbelieving heart that turns away
from the living God" (Hebrews 3:12). This spirit
of departing from Him is manifested by doubting
His Word because something else is wanted to
confirm it.

We need to have appropriating faith in regard to
His promises. We must make God's Word our
own personal possession.

A child was asked once what appropriating faith
was, and the answer was, "It is taking a pencil and
underlining the *mes* and *mines* and *mys* in the Bible." I don't know a better answer. It is saying,
"My Lord and my God." "He loved me and gave
himself for me." "I am my beloved's." It is standing isolated from everything, and feeling as if
there were no one anywhere but God and you. It
is claiming the largest share of His love for your-

self. This does not give offense to Him, but greatly pleases Him.

Put the power of God over against all the difficulties of life. Believe that He loves you today and is making the best out of everything for you forever. Take any word you please that He has spoken and say, "That is my word." Put your finger on this promise and say, "It is mine."

Disobedience

The last and greatest sin of the Israelites at this time was disobedience. This was shown in two ways. They refused to obey God and enter at once into the land, and they did afterward what God had not commanded them to do.

God had told them to go up and possess the land. They held back and disobeyed. The next morning they said. "We will go up now." But God said, "That would be disobedience a second time." He did not send them this time, and the result was that they were hurled back by the enemy. Whether we go or not, it must be as He commands. The minding of the Spirit is life, but the minding of the flesh is death.

When we obey the strong will in us, the self-directing force that is not subdued to God, we are always in the greatest peril. God calls it rebellion. How terribly He speaks of it later in the Bible, calling it "the rebellion, during the time of testing in the desert, where your fathers tested and tried me and for forty years saw what I did. That is why I was angry with that generation. . . . So I declared on oath in my anger, 'They shall never enter my rest' " (3:8-11). So the whole three million—men, women and children—were turned back into the desert to wander day after day, and year after year, panting from thirst, mothers seeing their children crying for water and having none to give them, and all eyes straining to catch a view of some green spot on the distant horizon. The blazing sun from a cloudless sky shone down constantly upon them, but still they went on, many falling sick by the way and leaving their ghastly skeletons to whiten on the sand.

No wonder Moses looked on and sang the mournful wail of the ninetieth Psalm, "You sweep men away in the sleep of death. . . . Who knows the power of your anger? For your wrath is as great as the fear that is due you" (90:5, 11).

And yet this spectacle is not half so sad as the strangely useless lives in the church today. Many young men who started out with glorious prospects of usefulness have had their lives blighted for many years because they have made some other things than God the idols of their heart. They will wake up at last to see that their lives have been wasted. They are saved, but oh, what they have missed because they were not brave enough to step out immediately at God's command and enter into all the blessings that would have followed their obedience. Great peace and joy were before them, but they turned from them.

Believe the picture given here to be true of what you, too, will become if you do not enter into rest.

Perhaps you are even now at the crisis hour of your life. God has led you up to this point and waits for your decision. Put aside everything that would lead you in the other direction, and dare to follow Jesus fully. Step out at once and be all the Lord's. Take care lest your refusal to do so may make this your day of provocation to God, and your life, too, becomes blighted. Blessings are waiting for you, and no hand but your own can push them aside, and no will but your own prevent their coming. God save you from refusing to enter into your purchased possession.

May the Holy Spirit Himself keep you from a rebellious heart! He will lead you and teach you if you are yielded to Him, and your self-will is laid down. God will perfect that which concerns you. The Lord bless you and lead you into the land of promise, and may you not ever seem to come short of it.

CHAPTER 4

Entering In

Moses my servant is dead. Now then, you and all these people, get ready to cross the Jordan River into the land I am about to give to them—to the Israelites. I will give you every place where you set your foot, as I promised Moses. (Joshua 1:2-3)

O ur subject leads us up to the gate of the land, not any longer to look over into it, but to enter upon it and possess it. It is as real an experience as the setting out from Egypt.

The steps for our entering into the promised land are very definite. First, Moses must die. The first sentence of the book of Joshua is: "Moses my servant is dead." The children of Israel could not go in as long as Moses was alive. He represented the law, and the law could never save any human being. There is in it no salvation either here or hereafter. The 10 commandments are not Christianity. They made nothing perfect, but the bringing in of a better hope did. They show us what we have to do but they cannot make us do it. Punishment never makes an offender do better. The example of a good man never has this effect. It is all law. We may try our best to do better, but we cannot. We may resolve and re-resolve, but at the end we are the same. All the efforts we can bring to bear upon our life and character will not make us good. That is the law.

Moses himself could not enter into the land; he was killed by his own law. He disobeyed, and so the Lord took him up into the heights of Pisgah and showed him the land unto which he could not enter. It is blessed to have the law and make a strong, clear stand upon the side of right, but we want more. Many people today are trying their best to keep, perhaps, a New Year's resolution to live a different life. But before the year is past, they fail. They do this over two or three times and finally give all up in despair. This is what the devil wants. He knew they would fail all the time. Many Christians are doing the same thing and perhaps think God has put them in hard places and their efforts are vain to live in them.

It is not what we can do, but what God can do. Jesus Christ came not to impose taxes but to pay them. He does not command you to be right; that was the work of Moses. The law says, "you must"; grace says, "I will enable you to do." The law says, "Be strong and be holy"; grace says, "I have come to bring you the blessings of holiness." The first words spoken to Joshua were: "Cross the Jordan River into the land I am about to give to them" (Joshua 1:2). Jesus comes to give, not to demand. He says, "My yoke is easy and my burden is light" (Matthew 11:30).

Holiness and Victory

Friend, have you passed from under the law into the blessed freedom of the gospel? Have you ceased from your own efforts and your best endeavors to do what is right? And have you received the full grace of the Blessed One so that He lives in you, keeping there the righteousness of the law so that while, in a sense, you are still living in the flesh you are walking after the Spirit?

Do not think we would depreciate the law in speaking of it thus, for it is as grand as it ever was. But we cannot keep it if we try our best. It is righteous but it can never make us righteous. Jesus has come to give us the power to keep it. A mirror will show us a dirty face but we cannot wash the stain off with the mirror. The law shows us the sin; Jesus gives us the cleansing from sin.

You will never get into the land of promise till you are through striving against sin, resisting the evil one, and laboring to be pure and holy apart from Christ. You must come to the Lord Jesus for Him to be in you holiness and victory.

God said, "Moses my servant," not, my son. While you are under the law you are only a servant. "To all who received him, to those who believed in his name, he gave the right to become children of God" (John 1:12). When you become as children, when you are really living in His bosom, then you have in you the very heart to do

His will. Because He has sent His Spirit into your heart, you can cry, "Abba, Father." Henceforth you are no more servants but sons, because you have within you the nature and life of God (see Romans 8:15-17).

Friend, God will give you this blessed experience. Come to Him; tell Him how you have striven to obtain it but cannot. Then believe that He gives it to you as a free gift and you will receive it. You will pass at once from the deep poverty of your baffled life into the possession of that blessed peace that surpasses all understanding. It is a blessed life, for there is not only the consciousness of His presence always in blessing, but there is both the will and power to do His will.

Not only must Moses die, but Israel must die also. "Now then, you and all these people, get ready to cross the Jordan" (Joshua 1:3). What is Jordan? The meaning of the type certainly is death and judgment. It is the act of putting off the past life, of stepping down into the floods of Jordan and coming out on the other side, as the Israelites did, not the same people any more. We are to go over Jordan, not stay in it. The past life is to be buried with its imperfections and its sins, and we are to go forth in resurrection life on the other side.

It is the figure of new life for the Christian heart. It is a definite committal of self in all its forms to the waves of death, and a parting with everything in this life that we ought not to have. It is saying good-bye to the world, to our past life and everything in our present life that is less than the will of God. It is a separation from the world, and a coming forth from this death as if we had dropped down from heaven, made over anew. Thenceforth we are citizens only of the heavenly world. "For you died, and your life is now hidden with Christ in God" (Colossians 3:3). "Those who belong to Christ Jesus have crucified the sinful nature with its passions and desires" (Galatians 5:24). There is now no dragging around of the old life or any efforts to make it better. We have something better, even Christ Himself, our life.

The Place of Death

In the Jordan River the Israelites built a pile of stones to mark the place of death (see Joshua 4:9). They built it there in the slime as a perpetual memorial of this fact. Then on the other side they built another heap of stones to mark the place where the dead were made alive. The one pile marked the death of sin, the other marked the new life in Christ.

This second experience of the resurrection life we must come into if we are to have abiding purity and victory. We must gather up what God condemns, what the Holy Spirit condemns, what our own sense of right condemns, and hand them over to death without one of them? They must die. We cannot kill them, but we can hand them over to God and give Him the right to slay. He will do it when they are completely given up to

Him. Then we are to seek His help to keep them from coming back.

The sacrifice must be bound to the horns of the altar, but we cannot do that either. We must give even that over to God. He will keep us. Our business is not with our old nature any longer. It may knock at the door and try to get in, but it must not be admitted. Paul speaks of it in this very language. He calls it "the old man" (Ephesians 4:22, KJV), referring to the mean, despicable nature we once had. When it is given over to God we are henceforth always to reckon it dead and under the flood of Jordan. And if we are dead with Him we will also live with Him.

Reckon from some special time when you died in Him. Build a pile of stones there to mark the spot. As certainly as you have handed over self and sin and all carnal desires to God, so certainly has He handed over His life and power and glory to you. Take it today, my friend. Build a heap of stones to mark the time, and never fight the old battle again. Christian life is not definite enough. We should not be dying and rising, and dying and rising again and again. We should build our memorial stones once for all, and then ever date from that time.

After the Israelites had passed over Jordan they were circumcised at Gilgal. This type of death to the flesh was even more vivid than the passing of the Jordan. It typified the handing over to God of the old, natural life and nature that you received at birth from your father and your mother. The apostle calls it flesh, and says it is to be slain.

It does not mean the body; there is nothing wrong in that in itself. The flesh means the natural character, not merely the physical life. It is the carnal mind that will not submit to the will of God. It includes the natural tastes, the esthetic pleasures, and all the desires that center upon self instead of upon God. It is centered in the will, in the mind, and in the tastes. It is not necessary to be a drunkard, or to be a glutton, or to be given up to earthly passion, to have a fleshly nature. There is a beautiful self that is full of culture. Many Christians are hindered by it from rising up into a true, spiritual life. Paul calls it the psychical man. It is fond of fine arts and refinement. Beautiful things have a keen fascination for it. A coarse and uncultivated nature will offend its finer tastes. All this is merely natural. It has nothing to do with the Spirit of God.

I asked a young man some time ago if he had received this heavenly Guest. His answer was, "I am not sure; sometimes I think I have, for when I hear fine music, now, it affects me more than it used to." He is not the only one who mistakes this taste for the Holy Spirit. The esthetic nature is not the spiritual oratory; eloquence may move the soul when the heart is far from God.

While the streets of Paris were flowing with blood during the Revolution, men and women were shedding tears every night in the theater over the fine acting that was given there. Often I have known cultivated taste to be a hindrance in the divine life, keeping people back from the position they ought to have taken, perhaps because some Christian did old things which they could not stand. We are not dead, beloved; the fleshly life has not left us if we are disturbed by these things. We must be dead to all kinds of flesh. It is not enough to slay what is apparently evil in us; the devil exalts when we stop with that. The psychical nature must be dead also.

We cannot even rejoice in the affections of the heart or the natural ties of human life until they are handed over to God and He has given them back to us as strong as they were before, but no longer selfish and earthly. This was the way with Abraham when he was able to offer up Isaac to God.

Dear friend, have you crossed the Jordan? Have you received the circumcision of the heart? Have you laid your whole throbbing self at the feet of your Lord, there to find yourself raised and filled with His life?

I heard of a warrior in ancient times, who, with his helmet and coat of mail on, pointed his sword at the breast of his child and sent it screaming in fright to its mother. The mother smiled and said, "My dear, that is only Papa." The father then took off his helmet and coat of mail, and with a smile pointed his sword again at the breast of his little one. The child rushed into his arms, and said, "I am not afraid of you now; I know you are my papa." So, beloved, may you rest in the arms of your Father without fear. And if He points His sword at any evil thing in you, let it go; He cannot hurt you. He will only slay the evil and let you lie there upon His breast and die in the arms of His love.

Fulfillment of the Word

The Israelites had to claim the fulfillment of His word. "Into the land I am about to give to them" (Joshua 1:2) was the command. He did not say the land that I will give them; that was the promise to Abraham. To Joshua it was, the land that I am about to give them this very day. The whole land was theirs, but they had to take it by one great claim.

It is well to understand the grammar of the Bible, especially its moods and tenses. There God can always be found. His great name is "I Am," not, "I Am Going to Be." That is the way all the promises come to us. He says to the sinner, "You are saved now if you accept the Lord Jesus as your Redeemer." He says to the weak Christian, "You are made whole by taking Me to be your sanctification." He says, respecting our prayers, "Believe that you receive the things you ask for and you will have them."

In the very moment we trust Him, God gives us the fullness of salvation, and afterwards it comes to us in detail. He gives it at once, but we enter upon the possession of it step by step. It is ours as fast as we go forward and step into it. Jesus Christ comes to you with all the blessings you can ever need in life, and offers all to you. If you accept it as all yours from the start, then you have to

go on and take it little by little, whether it is for-
giveness, sanctification, healing or power for service.

Not only did they have to claim their inheritance by faith, but they also had to step out into it.
"I will give you every place where you set your
foot, as I promised Moses" (1:3). They had received the promise of it before; now they must go
forward into it and place their feet upon it. The
King James puts the promise in the perfect tense,
and denotes an act just now completed: "that have
I given unto you." If we dare to place our foot
upon anything God has promised, He makes it
real to us. So, take Him as the supply for all your
needs, believe He is yours, and never doubt it
from this moment. Take the promise that suits
your need and step out on it, not touching it tim-
idly on tiptoe, but placing your foot flat down
upon it. Do not be afraid of it not holding your
weight. Put your whole need on the Word of the
eternal God for your soul, for your body, for your
work, for the dear ones for whom you are praying,
for any crisis in your life; then stand upon it forever.

Courage

The next step is courage. Make up your mind at
the beginning that the devil will frighten you if he
can, but make up your mind also not to be terrified by him. "Be strong and very courageous"
(1:7). He will be strength for you in the time of
conflict. Fear keeps many people out of the land of

promise. They are afraid of the sufferings they may have to endure, afraid of what someone may think or say, afraid of themselves.

Fear is the beginning of failure. God's word to Joshua about it was almost stern. "Have not I commanded you? Be strong and courageous. Do not be terrified; do not be discouraged" (1:9). He warns us about it all through the Bible. He took Jeremiah, weak as a woman and timid as a baby, and made him stand before kings and princes as a witness against them for fifty years. When Jeremiah tried to evade the difficult work, saying, "I do not know how to speak; I am only a child," the Lord rebuked him with this message: "Do not say, 'I am only a child.' You must go to everyone I send you to. . . . Get yourself ready! Stand up and say to them whatever I command you. Do not be terrified by them, or I will terrify you before them" (Jeremiah 1:6-7, 17).

If you get into the midst of a hard battle, the only thing to be done is to stand like flint against the enemy, and nothing will hurt you. It is always harder to run away. When Paul speaks of the different parts of the Christian armor, he mentions no defense that was provided for the back.

The next quality required was obedience. You should "obey all the law my servant Moses gave you" (Joshua 1:7). We are to go according to the Scriptures in everything, carefully adhering to all its commands. We are to observe to do them. This includes watchfulness and the careful study of their requirements. If we expect to make any progress in the higher life taught in the Scriptures, we must live according to the teachings of God's Word. They are not difficult to follow if we love them. It is easier to live a holy life than a wicked one. God has cast up a highway for His redeemed ones to walk in, and it is easier to stay there than to go back into sin.

It is not impossible to walk as He would have us, if we are watchful and obedient. His Spirit is ready to put these qualities within us if we will receive them. He expects us to have them. The minding of the flesh is death, but the minding of the Spirit is life and peace. The Holy Spirit seems to say to us, "Now mind me." It is not hard. The way of obedience is full of comfort and blessing. "If you are willing and obedient, you will eat the best from the land" (Isaiah 1:19).

"For the LORD your God will be with you wherever you go" (Joshua 1:9). He walks before you into the thickest of the conflict, and He is not going to let you fail. The watchword of the higher Christian life is, we are to give ourselves wholly to God and let him be all in all to us. We can count upon His presence. The secret of this life is "Christ in you, the hope of glory" (Colossians 1:27). He is not there as an influence but as a Person. It is as though a presence from another world had dropped down upon us and encompassed us with a world of light in which to go to heaven.

This is sometimes very different from the vain struggles of nature and the weary reaching out of this human heart after holiness. It is the holiness of another revealed within us and so shining out that we glorify not ourselves, but our Father in heaven. The Lord wants to make Himself thus real to us. He wants to become sufficient for all our needs. Has He become this to you? This is the land of promise. "This is eternal life: that they may know you, the only true God, and Jesus Christ, whom you have sent" (John 17:3).

May He make you lonesome for His presence, and show you your self and your need, until you cry, "[Lord,] if your Presence does not go with us, do not send us up from here" (Exodus 33:15). When you cry, the answer will come back; "My Presence will go with you, and I will give you rest" (33:14).

> Jesus, my Saviour, is all things to me,
> Oh, what a wonderful Saviour is He!
> Guiding, protecting, o'er life's troubled sea,
> Mighty Deliverer—Jesus for me.
>
> He is my Refuge, my Rock, and my Tower,
> He is my Fortress, my Strength and my
>   Power,
> Life Everlasting, my Daysman is He,
> Blessed Redeemer—Jesus for me.
>
> He is my Prophet, my Priest and my King,
> He is my Bread of Life, Fountain and
>   Spring,
> Bright Sun of righteousness, Day-Star is
>   He,

Horn of Salvation—Jesus for me.
    Jesus for me, Jesus for me,
    All the time, everywhere,
    Jesus for me.

CHAPTER 5

Overcoming

Joshua waged war against all these kings for a long time. Except for the Hivites living in Gibeon, not one city made a treaty of peace with the Israelites, who took them all in battle. For it was the LORD himself who hardened their hearts to wage war against Israel, so that he might destroy them totally, exterminating them without mercy, as the LORD had commanded Moses. (Joshua 11:18-20)

Be strong in the Lord and in his mighty power. Put on the full armor of God so that you can take your stand against the devil's schemes. For our struggle is not against flesh and blood, but against the rulers, against the authorities, against the powers of this dark world and against the spiritual forces of evil in the heavenly realms. Therefore put on the full armor of God, so that when the day of evil comes, you may be able to stand your ground. (Ephesians 6:10-13)

The first thought that arrests our attention, as we look at the children of Israel after they have really entered upon the land of promise, is the fact of conflict. The same thought must at once attract our notice as we look at Christians who have entered upon a higher experience in the land of rest.

One might suppose that all battles would be over after reaching such an experience, and that the Canaan of the soul must be a land entirely without conflict. Yet the apostle speaks of wicked spirits in the heavenly places, and wrestling with authorities and powers. We read of "the day of evil" in which we are to stand. Indeed, the nearer we get to the heavenlies the fiercer will be the foes. They are only to be overcome in the power of His might. No strength but that of the Lord can be sufficient to withstand them. There were no conflicts so terrible as those that met the Israelites on the Canaan side of the Jordan, at Jericho, at Ai, at Beth Horon, at the waters of Merom, and in all the battles by which the thirty-one kings of the land were at length subdued.

We know little of the power of temptation till we attempt to overcome it. We are not able to estimate the force of evil till we have attempted to match our strength against it and found we are not equal to the task of resisting it.

It is said that two Scotchmen were once talking on a beautiful Sabbath day, and one said to the other, "Do you never feel a temptation on these lovely Sabbaths to go out fishing? It is very hard for me to keep back from going." "No," said the other, "I never feel tempted; I just go." I believe there are too many in the world who yield just as easily and have an easy time because there is no struggle against sin. But let a man set his face like a flint for the truth and for the right and be determined, come what may, that he will not yield, and all the batteries of hell will be opened against him. He will find out soon enough that there is a personal devil.

A life of victory is not a life of freedom from the attacks of the enemy. He is always ready to spring upon us, and there can be no victory without conflict. The greater advances we make, the more will sin and Satan resist us. The nearer heaven we can get, the more of these wicked spirits we will meet. They throng the regions above us, and they are "authorities and powers." If we go on expecting peace, we will be unarmed to meet them. If we go armed for war, we will not be taken unawares, but will be armored and panoplied for victory.

The Captain of the Conflict

We must next look at the captain of this conflict. Before Joshua did any fighting he had a vision of his Captain. One night before the battle of Jericho he went out reconnoitering. He was looking over the defenses of the city, and, perhaps, arranging the plan of his attack. Suddenly, there flashed upon his vision the light of a flaming sword. Looking up he saw an armed warrior standing before his path. Joshua was no coward. Advancing with true soldier courage, he asked, "Are you for us or for our enemies?" (Joshua 5:13). Then there fell upon his ear a voice that thrilled his very soul, and that brought him pros-

trate to the earth in humility and adoration. "Neither, . . . but as commander of the army of the
Lord I have now come" (5:14). It was as if He
was saying, "You thought you were going to be
captain in this battle! That is My place. You
thought you were going to take Jericho. I am to
lead the forces, and you are but to follow Me.
'Take off your sandals, for the place where you
are standing is holy' (5:15)." And as Joshua
yielded up the command to this glorious Leader
he was led forward into victory.

The next place the army went up against was Ai.
And although God had marvelously given them victory through faith and simple obedience at Jericho,
Joshua sent spies up against this place to see how
strong its defenses were. There is no mention made
of any counsel being asked of the Lord. They used
human wisdom alone in reference to it and they
were ignominiously defeated. They were not following the Captain closely. The promise had been
given that if He were Leader, no man should be able
to stand before Joshua all the days of his life.

We are strong only when strong in Him. "We
are more than conquerors through him who loved
us" (Romans 8:37). We are commanded to be
"strong in the Lord and in his mighty power"
(Ephesians 6:10). We are not to take a little
strength from Him and rely a good deal upon our
own. We must be impotent in ourselves if we are
to have the Lord's help. When we are willing to lie
at the feet of Jesus and let Him lead all the battle,
we will be led to victory.

Joshua thought 3,000 men sufficient for Ai, and he did not even consult the Captain in this case. He would have been led in victory against this and against every foe if he had. It is the worst thing that can happen in our Christian life for us to trust ourselves. We need to come with Peter to the cross with downward head. When we get there the Lord can always lead us in triumph.

Victory in Faith

The victory in the land of promise is one of faith alone. This was God's first charge to Joshua, "Be strong and courageous" (Joshua 1:6). The whole book illustrates this principle, but especially the battle of Jericho. The author of the book of Hebrews speaks expressly of this. "By faith the walls of Jericho fell, after the people had marched around them for seven days" (Hebrews 11:30).

It must be faith that follows the leader. The priests and the people followed the ark; they did not go ahead of it. You cannot walk with God and yet do all the time as you please. We must see God's way and then follow. We must have a "Thus says the Lord" about things before we act. Some people seem to think all that is necessary is to have faith and they can claim anything they please. No, the will must be surrendered to God, and His Word must be accepted about all things before we will be able to believe them. We cannot risk our faith on the whims or caprices of ourselves or others. Let it be fixed on the eternal foundation of God's will and Word; then we shall not trust in vain.

Faith steps out after its leader. Faith can walk seven days around Jericho and not mind the rough places, and it can go seven times around on the seventh day. It is not dreamy; it is intensely actual. It goes forward putting its foot down firmly on every part of the promised land, following closely the footprints of the leader, not falling back or faltering till its march of victory is gloriously complete.

We must learn, too, the patience of faith that can wait for its possession and not be uneasy if it does not come right away. Seven days the Israelites waited for their victory, but did not falter. Perhaps the inhabitants of the city were watching them from the walls and making sport as they passed. But they marched on without being at all discouraged.

The first day there was no sign of victory, nor the second, nor the third, but on they marched in the confidence of faith. "You need to persevere so that when you have done the will of God, you will receive what he has promised" (10:36) "Though [the revelation] linger, wait for it; it will certainly come and will not delay" (Habakkuk 2:3). The note in the margin of my Bible reads, it will not tarry too long. The fulfillment may be protracted but it will not come too late.

There comes a time when faith not only expects but accepts the promise. The word comes at last: "the LORD has given you the city" (Joshua 6:16). Then faith sends up a shout that makes the earth and heaven ring, and marches in to its possession. "This is the victory that has overcome the world, even our faith" (1 John 5:4). In another place we

are told, "Do not throw away your confidence; it
will be richly rewarded" (Hebrews 10:35). There
is an allusion in this text to an ancient practice that
a soldier who threw away his shield could not
come back into the army. Cast not away therefore
your shield, the apostle says, for it has great recompense of reward. Only believe. Satan is a conquered foe and we need to always remember that
fact. Ephesians 6 is a great parallel with the book
of Joshua.

After Paul had mentioned the different pieces
of armor, he says above all, have the shield of
faith. This was a larger shield, large enough to
cover the whole person and armor too. God wants
you to have a great big faith that will cover all. He
has promised all, whether for soul or for body.
Our shield must be long enough to cover the 60
seconds in every minute, the 60 minutes in every
hour, all the hours in every day and all the days in
every year.

I am glad, however, that David had not only a
shield but a buckler—not only the large shield to
cover all the person, but a little one to fasten on the
arm and which could not be lost. Our faith in God
must not only be large, but it must be so fixed that
we cannot lose it. Then the enemy can have no
more power over us than he had over Christ.

The Secret of Failure

Faith has to learn also the secret of failure. It
was not always victory with Joshua, and it is not
always so in the highest Christian life. It ought to

be, but it is not. But the failure often brings wholesome lessons with it. The Lord often lets trouble come upon us as He did upon Peter, to let us get firmly established upon the rock. Do not be discouraged, dear friend, if you sometimes fail, even after you have reached high ground. Do not expect the failure, but if it comes, learn how to take the devil prisoner, and make him fight your battles for you. Learn such good lessons from the failure that the enemy will be afraid to touch you.

What have you been learning from your failures? Have they filled you with discouragement, or with vigilance and wisdom? Has it been true of you as Paul rejoiced that it was of the Corinthians, that "godly sorrow brings repentance that leads to salvation and leaves no regret, but worldly sorrow brings death. See what this godly sorrow has produced in you: what earnestness, . . . what alarm, what longing, what concern, what readiness to see justice done" (2 Corinthians 7:10-11). It has not been altogether an evil if it has made you more watchful, humble and holy. Do not be distressed about it, or moan and cry over it.

The LORD was not pleased with Joshua's morbid prayers and tears about the defeat at Ai, and He gave him a bracing word of kind reproof. "Stand up! What are you doing down on your face? Israel has sinned; they have violated my covenant, which I commanded them to keep. . . . Destroy whatever among you is devoted to destruction" (Joshua 7:10-12). When this command was obeyed, Israel was stronger than before. If you have failed in life, there is at the root some secret cause, something in your spirit with which God is not pleased.

Separation from God must follow till the sin is put away. He will not be with you any more until the accursed thing is removed. There is no use in attempting to fight the foe outside until the foe within the citadel is conquered. The heart needs to be laid open for the inspection of God. Be still before Him. Stop crying to the Lord to help you and say as David did, "Search me, O God, and know my heart; test me and know my anxious thoughts. See if there is any offensive way in me, and lead me in the way everlasting" (Psalm 139:23-24). When the sin is confessed and put away, God is always ready to restore the soul to His favor and deliver it from the power of evil. But there must be faithful work about it. If the sin remains, it will surely defeat you.

Two Fires

There are two fires in the spiritual world. One is the fire of the Holy Spirit that burns out the evil from the soul; the other is the unquenchable fire that burns and yet never consumes. Bless God that He lets you know about them before it is too late. The time is coming when we will be glad we have already found Him "a consuming fire." We are getting ready for that last great battle, and there is no discharge in that war. We are in the drill-room now, not ready yet for the conflict. But if we are true now, our Captain will not let us fail then. Failure here is not hopeless. Deal faithfully with the thing in you that wants to sin, and you will rise into new strength and victory.

In the next chapter, after Achan's sin, God told Joshua, "Do not be afraid; do not be discouraged. Take the whole army with you, and go up and attack Ai. For I have delivered into your hands the king of Ai, his people, his city and his land" (Joshua 8:1). The army won a glorious victory just where it had failed before. God led them over the same ground again, but this time it was in blessing.

Have you failed in a certain place in your life? Be sure you will be tested in that same place again. You cannot go on till you have had victory there. The same thing will meet you until there has been such a triumph over it that it can never trouble you any more. You cannot go on and leave Ai behind. Only be true. God's Word will not fail you, and you will yet be able to look back over your whole life and say, "Not one word has failed of all the good promises he gave" (1 Kings 8:56).

The Higher Lessons

Then there are deeper and higher lessons for the conflict to be learned afterwards. Joshua had not only to meet the open attacks of the enemy, but he had to encounter their wiles. The devil comes in disguise sometimes and deceives the children of God and lures them into sin.

After Joshua had won the victory at Ai, there came to him a deputation of the queerest people he had yet seen. They were dressed in old clothes, their shoes were worn out, and they were covered with dust. They looked like a company of modern tramps. They represented themselves as tired pilgrims who had come from a long distance, and whose bread was moldy and their water gone. They asked Joshua to give them shelter, and they would become hewers of wood and drawers of water for his people. Joshua listened to his good-natured impulse, and, without inquiring of the Lord about it, made a league of peace with them.

Very soon he found, to his horror, that they were his near neighbors and inhabitants of the land, whom the Lord had told him to exterminate. He had listened to the voice of worldly and human sympathy, and had not gotten divine counsel. But his word could not be broken, and the league had to stand. However, these people became an endless source of evil to Israel afterward, teaching them lessons about idolatry and opening the way for those forbidden alliances and intermarriages that afterward were so ruinous to their spiritual life.

If the devil cannot cause you to fall in open conflict, he will send his emissaries, disguised as angels, to deceive you. Perhaps it will be to make you act quickly from your own impulses, and sometimes make a decision in this way that will be a snare for life are that will bring you many a heartache in the future. Many have acted thus quickly and brought trials which have caused them to go mourning all their days. Sometimes it is a partnership in business, or a social friendship, or a more intimate alliance. God only is able to detect the evil in these things.

There are foolish things that cause us to trip in 10,000 places. We fall into them by having wrong views of life, and taking for good that which is really evil because we did not go to the Lord and ask light from Him about it. We sit in judgment on others. We decide matters by our hasty ideas of what is right. We sympathize with people and think we are doing them good. The only secure place to be is in constant communication with Him who has said, "In all your ways acknowledge him, and he will make your paths straight" (Proverbs 3:6). "He guides the humble in what is right and teaches them his way" (Psalm 25:9). The soul that is wholly yielded to Him and is afraid of taking a step alone will walk safely. The devil may come to such a soul with ten thousand flattering devices, but he cannot win it from the path of safety and victory.

Into the Christian life come occasions that Paul calls "the day of evil"—pitched battles when the heavens are black and the earth is responding with the tramp of the oncoming foe. Your little force is shut in on all sides, and there seems no chance of deliverance. Such were the battles of Beth Horon and Merom, when all the kings of Palestine met, determined to crush out the invaders. Joshua met these fierce bands with steady courage. Not waiting for them to attack him, he stepped out in faith and attacked them. Finding the day not long enough for the battle, he called upon the sun and moon to halt in the heavens, and the day was lengthened out until he had finished his victory.

We, too, have critical conflicts to meet in life, when all the forces of the evil one seem to combine for our destruction. Such a Gethsemane comes in every life, and perhaps leaves some of God's dear children with a feeling that they have lost very much by not standing steadily in it. God will give you grace to hold your ground. Even there you can stand out in His strength and power and be able to bring glory to Him by a successful resistance. He sees the battle and will give the power to be victorious. We little know how much may hang on the result of these conflicts. Often the conflict comes in the closet hour.

There are many battles where I think I know what Paul meant when he said, "We have been made a spectacle to the whole universe, to angels as well as to men" (1 Corinthians 4:9). From the air around us there are millions of glorious beings looking down upon these issues. If they are lost, even upon the brow of the dear Redeemer there must come a blush of shame, but a shout of delight from hosts of devils who also are spectators.

Do not look upon these conflicts as unimportant. Years of service for the Master have been the outcome of more than one such moment, though no one but God alone knew the battle had been fought. If you have not passed through them, they will surely come. But God has promised to be your strength, your rock, and the arm of your power. As you trust that mighty power in the fiercest attacks, you will find it all-sufficient. The day will come when you will be able to raise the victor's song: "Thanks be unto God, which always causeth us to triumph in Christ" (2 Corinthians 2:14, KJV).

We learn the still more important lesson that life has not only its long campaigns. "Joshua waged war against all these kings for a long time. Except for the Hivites living in Gibeon, not one city made a treaty of peace with the Israelites" (Joshua 11:18-19). When the 31 kings were are all subdued, then the land had rest from war. We have enlisted not for one Gettysburg, but for the whole period of conflict. Do not think you have one or two sharp battles merely; they will come again and again. We cannot have rest from war until all 31 kings are subdued. With not one of our enemies should we be willing to make peace.

The city that Joshua made a compact with was afterwards a curse to Israel. "It was the LORD himself who hardened their hearts to wage war against Israel, so that he might destroy them totally" (11:20). It was the only way of safety for the Israelites. How could they be destroyed unless they were led into conflict? The only way the Lord can destroy the evil in us is by letting it come out and show itself to us. These hard places we come to so often in life are of the Lord. He is deeply interested in the slaying of the evil.

The land is not subdued in a day. We read in Ephesians that we are not only to withstand in the evil day, but having done all, to stand. Then we will be able to say with Paul at last, "I have fought the good fight, I have finished the race, I have kept the faith. Now there is in store for me the crown of righteousness, which the Lord, the righteous Judge, will award to me on that day" (2 Timothy 4:7-8).

Let us take this lesson of perseverance, and go out trustfully to meet the things that surely will oppose us. Let the poetry of the subject go. Let the glow of the inspired feeling give place to the downright reality. Go forth with a watchful heart, but without fear. The difficulties will not be too hard. He is able for your battles. It is always true, "God is faithful; he will not let you be tempted beyond what you can bear. But when you are tempted, he will also provide a way out so that you can stand up under it" (1 Corinthians 10:13). "I will know that you stand firm . . . without being frightened in any way by those who oppose you. This is a sign to them that they will be destroyed, but that you will be saved—and that by God" (Philippians 1:27-28).

I'm more than conqueror through His
    blood,
  Jesus saves me now;
I rest beneath the shield of God,
  Jesus saves me now.
I go a kingdom to obtain,
I shall through Him the victory gain,
  Jesus saves me now.

Before the battle lines are spread,

Jesus saves me now;
Before the boasting foe is dead,
    Jesus saves me now.
I win the fight, though not begun,
I'll trust and shout, still marching on,
    Jesus saves me now.

I'll ask no more that I may see,
    Jesus saves me now;
His promise is enough for me,
    Jesus saves me now.
Though foes be strong and walls be high,
I'll shout, He gives the victory,
    Jesus saves me now.

Why should I ask a sign from God?
    Jesus saves me now;
Can I not trust the precious blood?
    Jesus saves me now.
Strong in His Word, I meet the foe,
And, shouting, win without a blow,
    Jesus saves me now.

Should Satan come like 'whelming waves,
    Jesus saves me now;
Ere trials crush, my Father saves,
    Jesus saves me now.
He hides me till the storm is past,
For me He tempers every blast,
    Jesus saves me now.

CHAPTER 6

Inheriting

When Joshua was old and well advanced in years, the LORD said to him, "You are very old, and there are still very large areas of land to be taken over." (Joshua 13:1)

So Joshua said to the Israelites: "How long will you wait before you begin to take possession of the land that the LORD, the God of your fathers, has given you?" (18:3)

The land of promise is not a place of ceaseless conflict. There comes a time when we enter on that which we have conquered and really possess that which we have claimed.

What is meant by possessing the land? There are two thoughts suggested by the term. First, we are to appropriate the land, that is, make it our own. Then we are to sit down and occupy it.

The personal pronoun *my* expresses the first of these acts. You have what is your own. You need no interpreter on that subject. What is yours you take a strange interest in. The little cottage in the forest, that poor deformed child, are far more to you than all the world, because they are your own.

It is in this way you are to make the promises your own. The Bible is to be read as if written expressly for you. Jesus is loved because He is your blessed Savior. The Holy Spirit is your own personal Sanctifier, belonging to no one as He does to you. God is your own God, to be used for all things for which you need Him. The promises are made yours by appropriating faith. You rejoice in them in hope, and soon you find they are really yours in blessed experience. After that you go on into actually living them out. There are many things we believe in for Christian life, but have never entered into by realizing that they fully belong to us.

The root of the word *possessing* means *to sit down upon*. We are not to step over into our inheritance once in a while, but we are to settle down upon it. We must live and know all there is in the possibilities of Christian life. This is as blessed in the workshop as in the sanctuary, as true down at the foot of the mountain with the foaming demoniac as upon the height where Jesus was transfigured and heaven poured down its celestial glory upon the bewildered disciples. It is blessed thus to enter upon this possession and find it practical and real. Have you gone on to possess the land? Have you not only claimed and conquered it, but are you living in it?

Given by Promise

What is meant by the inheritance? First, Israel's inheritance was given them by promise. So our inheritance is all the fullness of God's exceedingly great and precious promises: all the unclaimed wealth of these 40,000 checks in the Bank Book of the Bible-promises for the soul, promises for the body, promises for ourselves, promises for others, promises for our work, promises for our trials, promises for time and promises for eternity.

Next, Israel's inheritance was given on account of Abraham. So our inheritance has been purchased by the Lord Jesus Christ. It includes all for which He died. There are redemption rights, for which He has paid the full, the tremendous price. We should be willing that no part of that mighty purchase should go by default or be lost to us. Did He die for our own sins and rise again for our justification? Then justification is our redemption right. Did He bear our sicknesses and carry our infirmities? Then it is all right to lay them upon Him. Is it true that "because by one sacrifice he has made perfect forever those who are being made holy" (Hebrews 10:14)?

Then by that one perfect sacrificial offering we have the right to claim our sanctification. Has He received from the Father all the fullness of grace, power and holiness for those who abide in Him? Then these are our rights of inheritance. Has He sent down from heaven the gifts and presence of the Holy Spirit? Then we may claim all His fullness of grace and power for ourselves. It is the children's bread, and let us not fear to take our place at the Father's table. There is bread enough and to spare; why should we perish with hunger?

Israel's inheritance was given on account of Abraham. So our inheritance has been bestowed on account of the Lord Jesus Christ. The patrimony of each was distinct. The land was equitably divided among them by a prescribed divine plan, and according to the allotment of the will of God. So our inheritance in Christ is an individual one. To each of us Christ gives our own salvation, sanctification, Christian experience and special service. No one should wish to copy another's life. God has for every true soul "a white stone with a new name written on it, known only to him who receives it" (Revelation 2:17). Just as the same sun will shine on your garden and produce a little blue-eyed violet in one place, and in another a gorgeous rose, and elsewhere a pure white lily of the valley, so Christ develops in every soul according to its kind. He would have all to be as varied as the flower of the field and the stars of the sky.

Divine Apportionment

Our inheritance, like theirs, is a matter of divine apportionment. The gifts of the Holy Spirit are not all bestowed upon one, but "all these are the work of one and the same Spirit, and he gives them to each one, just as he determines" (1 Corinthians 12:11). He exercises a loving oversight in His blessings. And, while He freely gives to all who ask and trust Him, and the only limitation in the measure of our blessings is our own faith and obedience, yet even when He gives most largely it is in the line which His wisdom and love see most consistent with our highest good and His supreme glory.

What does God mean by the complaint, "There are still very large areas of land to be taken over" (Joshua 13:1), and "How long will you wait before you begin to take possession of the land" (18:3)? It implies much neglect and failure on our part. The apostle says, "Therefore, since the promise of entering his rest still stands, let us be careful that none of you be found to have fallen short of it" (Hebrews 4:1). He is speaking of the land of promised rest as a land of realization and of blessed victory over enemies, foreshadowed by Canaan. He bids us fear, not that we will miss it altogether, but come short of it, that is, not quite receive all its promises. We may miss it by just a little, and fail, perhaps, by a hairline of fully reaching all that it means.

Do you possess all the land about which you know? There has been a great deal promised, but is it all yours by actual possession? "Now that you know these things, you will be blessed if you do them" (John 13:17). A brother told us one night that God would not let him say a certain grace was his own without putting him in a place where he would have to show it before the week was over. Whatever you know about Christian truth, God will make you put in practice. Many of you have been studying this subject of Christian holiness. Have you lived it out? Are you coming up in daily practice to what you know about it?

Have you received all that you have believed for, or are you talking about having it by faith, but have not really had it given to you yet? Faith is the substance of the possession; it is not a sham. It is the evidence of things not seen. We often hear Christians say, "I have victory by faith, but I have not the evidence yet." Then you do not have the faith, for faith is the evidence. It is a deep, inwrought conviction, coming to you right from the heart of God, that the thing you have believed for is yours. Have you thus entered on that which you have believed for?

Have you come up to all the meaning of God's words and promises to you? We are easily satisfied with a little, without all that there is in the promises. We limit them and so limit Him, and we lose much of the blessing that would be ours if we did not so dwarf them to the miserable level of our indolence or fears.

Are you coming short in any particular of God's blessed will and purpose for you? Are you fulfilling Second Thessalonians 1:11? "That our God may count you worthy of his calling, and that by his power he may fulfill every good purpose of yours and every act prompted by your faith."

God has a will for us. There is a lofty ideal in His heart for each one. Are we coming short of it? We cannot fail His conception for our life without disappointing Him. If we do come short of the Holy Spirit's peace for us, it will be vain to make spiritual progress without it. There can be no forward movement until His will is first met. If He has been saying to us, "Come up higher," we must obey before there can be any blessing in any other direction.

The High Consciousness of the Call

The high consciousness of this call of God in the heart is often a sad contrast to the miserable experience of failure the life represents. Men are afraid or reluctant to obey it, especially if it be in the direction of leaving off something that is dear to them. The apostle says, "Not that I have already obtained all this, or have already been made perfect, but I press on to take hold of that for which Christ Jesus took hold of me" (Philippians 3:12). Paul felt a hand upon him pressing him on; he knew it was God's hand, and he was fully meeting it.

Are you abreast with God, my friend? He will not lead you forward faster than you are able to go. He knows all the depths of human weakness, but His high ideal reaches down to every part of it. God lets down to you as much light as you can live by today. There will come brighter, clearer revelations tomorrow. If today's light is missed, tomorrow's cannot be received. There is never light enough to see very far ahead. It is given only as you use it.

Have you missed opportunities for work, which will one day be silent witnesses against you? Will any souls be lost through your failure? Have there been any openings in the providence of God into which you have not entered? There is no use in seeking more supplies of grace for Him, while there remains so much land to be possessed.

The Church's Failure

It is a very sad fact, and I believe it is typical of the state of Christianity today, that seven whole tribes of Israel failed for a time to enter into their possession. They held back from the self-denial, and remained encamped around the tabernacle of Shiloh. There was no progress there. It seems to foretell the mournful truth that the Church would one day lie down in supreme indifference to much that Jesus died and rose again to secure for her. She is not pressing forward into her possession. It seems to hint that even yet the great mass of Christians are coming short of their inheritance.

This is not true of all, but there are many disciples who go for years and years without even the assurance of salvation. Indeed it is a rare thing to find in many quarters. They think it is presumption to say they have such assurance. If you should ask in any ordinary Christian gathering how many were living whole lives, overcoming temptations day by day, and enabled by Christ's power to follow in His will according to all the light that has been given, you would find multitudes who would hesitate to make such a confession. I have been able to count on my fingers in some places the Christians who would dare to say so.

This is sad. The least inheritance in the land of promise means full salvation. The Church needs to be roused up from its sleep of centuries, from the low standard of Christian life that it has accepted and that makes a life of holiness such a wonder. It is deemed exceptional to find such lives as Fletcher, or Wesley, and other saintly lives. It ought to be the rule. Faith like Franke's or George Mueller's is considered a prodigy in the spiritual world, but God expects all His people to believe Him perfectly.

The epistles speak of all Christians as saints. The letter to the Corinthians was addressed to such. They were all "called to be saints" (1 Corinthians 1:2, KJV). "All the saints salute you" (2 Corinthians 13:13, KJV), Paul says in another place. God expects nothing less of us. "Follow my example, as I follow the example of Christ" (1 Corinthians 11:1), was the apostle's direction. God expects us to be pure and holy up to our knowledge of His requirements, and to know and do the full measure of His will.

This is the land upon which it is our privilege to enter. These are the possibilities that are placed before us. All may secure them, for the land was the common inheritance of all the tribes. There were special prizes beyond this claimed in it by Joshua, Caleb and a few others. And there are still some brave spirits in the Church who gain special crowns of victory as rewards of unusual faith and service. But the ordinary inheritance of every Christian should be at least a full salvation.

Do not excuse yourself from receiving this by any false humility. Do not talk about "not expecting ever to be a saint." If you are willing simply to get into heaven, as Job says, by the skin of your teeth, the Lord help you. There will be crowds there at the gate just like you, and whether they will ever get in is doubtful. I am sure at least they will so block the way that it will be a long time before you will see the gate. I do not believe the soul is saved at all that is satisfied to miss any of God's blessings, or that does not care whether or not it brings glory to God during its earthly life.

God hates sin and wants to overcome, and any Christian who can sit down to ease, not caring whether his spiritual life is gaining in power, had better look into the matter of his conversion. Perhaps he will find he is a backslider. The apostle says, "be careful that none of you be found to have fallen short" (Hebrews 4:1). It is a fearful thing for a Christian to be willing to be half saved. He is in tremendous peril. His life should be a constant growth, a continual pressing out after new attainments.

The Cause of Failure

What was the cause of the Israelites coming short of their full inheritance? One cause is hinted at in the expression. "How long will you wait to take possession of the land that the LORD, the God of your fathers, has given you" (Joshua 18:3). The word implies that they were indolent, and quite satisfied with their present condition. There was lack of holy energy and aspiration after the inheritance promised. They were taking things easy.

They were little concerned about failure and sin. They would have gone on forever in their present state of apathy and distaste for conflict. They were breathing the atmosphere of the enchanted ground.

Have you ever, perhaps even while on your knees, had such an influence thrown over you—the very soothing balm of Satan, who would thus lull your spiritual senses to sleep? How it has made you shrink from the pain of holy inspiration, and made you willing to fall back into a passive contentment! God is calling you to press forward, to "throw off everything that hinders" (Hebrews 12:1); and "do not . . . become lazy, but . . . imitate those who through faith and patience inherit what has been promised" (6:12).

Is this your spiritual state, friend? If not, ask the Lord to awaken you out of your sleep. There may come a very terrible awakening some day if you do not. He may have to strike the chords of deep anguish to awaken you out of this sleep of death.

Timidity was another cause of failure. They dreaded meeting the foes that were still in the land, and so left them unconquered.

They failed also because the majority hung back. Nearly all Israel was encamped around Shiloh. It was a lonely thing to step out into the regions beyond, and they shrank from it. As long as the larger number of the people stood back, the rest were contented to be as they. We have got to step out from the majority. The path of life is "a narrow road with here and there a traveler." God help us to be singular, if that is necessary. Better to have God on our side, whether we be in the majority or the minority.

They were hindered also by a spirit of self-complacency. Their past history they counted a good enough record. This increased their spiritual apathy. Martin Luther said, "If thou say 'enough,' thou shalt perish." We have not got enough until we have received all His will. Yesterday's victories were only for yesterday. Count not that you have already attained, but press on for all the fullness of His blessed will.

What meaning is there for us in God's tender appeal to Joshua, "How long will you wait before you begin to take possession of the land" (Joshua 18:3)? Is He asking any of you, "How long are you going to remain unsanctified?"—until some terrible trial wakes you up, or some fearful fall makes you realize your condition? Or, are you waiting for death to do that work within you? That is a poor time to be saved, and a poorer one to be sanctified, when the mind is clouded by the power of disease. How long are you slack to possess the land?

Do It Now

Now, while your brain is clear and your choice is not compelled, make the wise choice, and give yourself wholly to God. Use all the light He has given you. Let not your inheritance go by default. Let not the grace of God be received in vain. There is not a promise He has made but He is anxious to make good to you. The alluring visions of grace and glory He has held before you, He will transcribe upon your heart and engrave deeply into your whole life if you will let Him. There is not a crown hung up in heaven's mansions that is not going to be worn by somebody. Do not let these dreams become a mockery to you. They may be real, and God wants them to be real for you. He has a separate inheritance for each one. You cannot get into mine, and I cannot get into yours. Do not fail to enter upon yours. If you do, you will suffer eternal loss, even if you do not lose your soul.

The day will soon come when you, too, will be old and stricken in years. Time is rushing by; God has not given you a day too many. Suppose they should stop tomorrow, and you never have another opportunity to gain a victory for Him. You would give all the world for a chance to resist temptation, or for another hard place in which to glorify God as you had before dishonored Him. The days once gone can never come back. You will not pass this way again.

There will be no chance in heaven to learn holiness, to have patience with unholy people, or to love your enemies. There will be no enemies to love. If you do not have grace enough here to learn these lessons, there will be no other chance for it. This is the only place in which you can be a soldier, or endure suffering, or show forth the graces of sanctification in trial. You have abundant opportunity for that now. If there were no giants on the hill there would be no inheritance for you to gain. Caleb would never have won his crown if it had not been for the Anakim. He met them in the name of God and conquered them, and Hebron became significant as the place of fellowship and the friendship of God.

If you find difficulties in your home, or enemies in your own heart, or trouble anywhere in your life, God has given them to you as opportunities for victory. There you will find the crown of glory and the land of promise. It is always the place where God plants His paradises; Eden is always in the midst of a wilderness; the place of springs is always upon the barren mountains. It is the desert of life that is to be made to blossom like a rose.

When God wanted to build a temple, He first sent Abraham to purify the place by the consecrated offering of Isaac. Then it was again used as a place of sacrifice at the threshing-floor of Araunah. After that God could use it as the place of His sanctuary. When He wanted a capital, He sent David to take a hill so difficult to capture that its inhabitants laughed at him and defended it with the blind and lame. Yet David conquered it, and it became the Zion of the Lord, the holiest, dearest place in all the world forever.

Go out into the field where He has cast your lot. Meet the temptations and difficulties in the strength of the Lord and turn them into Edens. In that way you show forth to others, through them, the grace of Jesus Christ and the power of a consecrated life. You do not need to go into the land that is very far off to do this, for the opportunity is very near you.

May He send you forth to gain all this large inheritance and give you the joy of saying at last, "Not one word has failed of all [His] good promises" (1 Kings 8:56).

> Transform us! Let us bear
> Thine image everywhere,
> The living witness of the living Word.
>
> We would in Thee abide,
> In Thee be glorified,
> And shine as candles lighted by the Lord.
>
> Jesus, in us fulfill
> Thine ever blessed will!
> We breathe a glad "amen" to Thy decree.
> We would henceforth entwine
> Our darkened lives with Thine,
> Nor ever find the selves we lose in Thee.

CHAPTER 7

Choice Possessions

If I speak in the tongues of men and of angels, but have not love, I am only a resounding gong or a clanging cymbal. If I have the gift of prophecy and can fathom all mysteries and all knowledge, and if I have a faith that can move mountains, but have not love, I am nothing. If I give all I possess to the poor and surrender my body to the flames, but have not love, I gain nothing.

Love is patient, love is kind. It does not envy, it does not boast, it is not proud. It is not rude, it is not self-seeking, it is not easily angered, it keeps no record of wrongs. Love does not delight in evil but rejoices with the truth. It always protects, always trusts, always hopes, always perseveres.

Love never fails. But where there are prophecies, they will cease; where there are tongues, they will be stilled; where there is knowledge, it will pass away. . . .

And now these three remain: faith, hope and love. But the greatest of these is love. (1 Corinthians 13:1-8, 13)

99

There are some special possessions spoken of in the book of Joshua, besides the common inheritance of the land. These were meant to illustrate the special possessions that we may still obtain through courage, faith and obedience.

Possessed by Courage

We have, first, an account of the taking of Hebron by Caleb. A few years after they entered the land, when the conquest of the great kings had been completed and the Israelites were in possession, Caleb came to Joshua. He asked for the fulfillment of a promise made to him by Moses more than forty years before, that he should have the city of Hebron for his inheritance. It was a place sacred to the people by many associations. It had been the home of Abraham and near it was the cave of Machpelah in which were the graves of their forefathers.

It was a place of natural beauty, surrounded by a valley of great fertility, and was one of the chief cities of Canaan, older indeed than even the oldest city in Egypt. Caleb had set his heart upon it when he had gone through the land with the spies, and Moses promised that it should be his as soon as they entered upon their inheritance. The rebellion of the tribes turned them back into the desert. Yet, though Caleb had to wait half a century for it, he did not despair. He knew he should have his inheritance. The long years of waiting were now over. As soon as it was fitting that he should present a personal request, Caleb asked that the promise given so long ago should be redeemed.

It was not an easy possession to take, and he was now an old man of 85; yet he was as strong as on the day he left Egypt both to go out and to come in. To gain his possessions he must drive out the giant Anak who was then its ruler. Later, the city became David's capital, and still later it became the home of Elizabeth, and John the Baptist was probably born in the neighborhood.

But dear as Hebron is to the Bible student historically, the lessons connected with it on account of the significance of its name are still more precious. The word means "friend" and it is significant of our spiritual inheritance of fellowship and love. It is a choice spiritual inheritance, the highest of all the victories of grace-love. Paul says love is the greatest of all the graces, and superior to all other spiritual gifts.

After Caleb had gained possession of Hebron, another special inheritance was gained by Othniel, one of the brave leaders of the same tribe. His name means the "lion of God." He claimed an old literary city in the neighborhood of Hebron and Kiriath Sepher. The civilization of some of those ancient kingdoms was as remarkable as our own. They had splendid libraries, with thousands of volumes, many of them works on philosophy and natural science.

Kiriath Sepher was the City of Books. Literature, schools and colleges probably flourished there. It was doubtless the seat of instruction about the Canaanitish worship. Caleb promised his daughter to any one who would take Kiriath Sepher. Othniel said at once, "I will take it!" He went forth with the same faith in God that Caleb showed, conquered the enemy, took the city, and won Acsah for his bride (Joshua 15:16-17). It, too, is the type of spiritual blessings, as Hebron was of love. Kiriath Sepher is significant of truth. It represents our deliverance from spiritual blindness and the old carnal mind with all its foolish ideas. It means taking Christ's thought in everything, and possessing the illumination of the Spirit. Hebron is the place of love, Kiriath Sepher of light and truth.

Connected with all this story is a romance of singular beauty, that is very suggestive of other spiritual truths. Othniel had won his bride, and with her came a splendid inheritance, but it had one very serious defect. The land lay facing the south, exposed to the scorching heat of a tropical sun, and there was no water on it. Then Acsah, as she came to her husband, petitioned her father that, as he had given her a rich inheritance which yet had no springs upon it, he would give her also a spring of water. Caleb gave her the "upper and lower springs" (15:19).

From the upper spring the hillside could be irrigated. By pipes the water could be carried along the ridge of the hill and liberated there at will, and the burning and arid sands could thus be changed into a very garden of fertility. The lower spring would irrigate the valley in the same way. Springs

in the valleys are very unusual. They are fre-
quently found in mountains, but not often in the
valleys. The word Achsah means grace. The prize
Othniel won by giving up his natural wisdom was
grace, suggesting the complete fullness of God's
grace.

What is the meaning of all these types to us?
The first is that our very choicest inheritance, the
highest place we can possibly take in the land, is
the place of love. When we enter the land of Canaan the first thing we must do is to stand in the
place of faith with Joshua. But, when the battles
are over and we are ready to sit down in our possession, there comes another experience, typified
by the taking of Hebron.

The battle of Jericho was a victory of faith; the
capture of Hebron was a victory of love. We overcome by faith; we remain overcomers through
love. Faith may indeed remove mountains, but
faith without love is like a resounding gong or a
clanging cymbal. I have seen Christians who have
had a wonderful experience in the line of faith, but
who seemed to have no love, and their lives have
been blighted by that lack. You may be able to
take Jericho and conquer the kings at Beth Horon,
but you will fail if you do not win Hebron and
slay the sons of Anak.

Sometimes it seems as if God were leading only
to the development of the experience of faith, and
there are few calls for the higher grace of love.
Then it seems as if the school of love were suddenly opened and all the testings are in that line,

and the scholar is learning such lessons as these: Love "is not rude, it is not self-seeking, it is not easily angered, it keeps no record of wrongs" (1 Corinthians 13:5). If this experience has not come to you yet, dear friend, be sure it will meet you before God is through with you. If it has not come, your experience is like the barren rocks where there are no springs of water, the very essence of God and heaven. Love is to cover the sides with green growth. Love is the fulfilling of the law. If you are willing to be overcomers in this field you may walk ever with a glowing heart and a sweet and loving spirit, and without these all else is worse than vain.

A Divine Love

This love must be divine. It is not our natural spirit or affection springing up in the heart. It is not something that we can compel by our own will. You must feel the lack of it, and lie down prostrate at the foot of the cross. Then God will baptize you into it by pouring into you the very nature and spirit of Christ Himself.

It is not man's love, it is God's love put in the heart by the Holy Spirit. If you try to get it in any other way, you will find how helpless you are in this direction. You will come sharp up against people whom you will find it impossible to love. God has meant you to fail in it to show you the weakness of your own fancied strength in this very matter. You are deeply ashamed of the failure, and see, too, that if you are not victorious here you perhaps have no certain hope of salvation. You become painfully aware of the necessity of having love for them, and see also the perfect helplessness of your heart to give it. Then you will finally humble your proud self, and be ready at last to have the spirit of love within you.

How sweetly then He comes, changing Boanerges into John the loving disciple who rests on Jesus' bosom!

Hebron is the stronghold of Canaan. It is the citadel of the Lord. The things that were most opposed to God in your spiritual nature may be most fully consecrated to Him, and you become strongest for Him where you were the strongest for the devil, so that men will say, how wonderful is the grace of God!

You may think this spirit of gentleness and love is not your nature. Of course it is not. We all come to a place where all our nature revolts against love, especially to the unloving, but God has made it easy. He will not let you off without it. He will not, because He has it for you. Are you going to take Hebron, dear friend? The Anakim may be mighty, but by God's help you can drive them out.

The Spirit of Self

Hebron is called Kiriath Arba, or the city of Arba. Arba was the father of Anak, and Anak had three sons—all giants like himself. It will help us out a little to look at the meaning of their names. If you think it is too fanciful you can let it go. The truth is not fanciful even if the frame is. The name Arba suggests the spirit of self-will, that thing in you that wants to be master.

Arba was the type of the spirit of self, and the victory of Caleb over him was the victory of love over selfishness. Self does not appear so strongly at the beginning of the Christian life. You find it a long way in, after sin has been slain for years. The Israelites had left Egypt more than 40 years previously. Even when sin has been slain, self remaining in the heart must be brought into subjection to God. All that we call natural strength, even what is usually termed "the better self," must be laid upon the altar. Old Arba, giant of self-will, must be slain and the will of God brought into the soul in his place.

The love of God is not an emotion of ecstatic feeling. This is often manifested by people whose love breaks down upon little provocation. God does not care so much for effervescent joy as for a will that chooses His will and holds to it in the very teeth of temptation. This is called in the Word "a perfect heart" (Psalm 101:2, KJV). It stands firmly with the hand on the helm, the will fixed, and the eye on God. The life will not be all an easy holiday, but there will be in it what is far better, a faithful living up to the requirements of God and a constant sense of living always in the city of Hebron, the place of His unclouded presence.

Arba had three sons, and their names are also typical of evil. The first of these was Anak. His name meant "long-necked." Do you know what that means? A long-necked animal holds its head very high and looks down on things below it. There are some professing Christians who have such necks. It is the spirit of pride that God hates. He loves the meek and humble spirit, but He knows the proud far off. "I live in a high and holy place, but also with him who is contrite and lowly in spirit" (Isaiah 57:15).

If you are to dwell in Hebron, Anak must die. The long neck must be hewed off by the sword of Christ. What is the principal thing that hinders our love from going out to other people? It is our abominable pride. You measure yourself with them and seem in your own eyes better than they. Measure yourself with God instead, and learn how you appear in His sight. Then see how abominable a thing your pride is, and never venture to criticize a human being again. Job got right with God when he got a view of himself. "Therefore," he says, "I despise myself and repent in dust and ashes" (Job 42:6).

How sweetly Christ linked together love and humility by getting down and washing the disciples' feet. This was a lowly service, but He was not ashamed of it. The spirit of lowliness is the spirit of love. If you have it you will not be able to see the spots in other people's lives. The critical eye sees them very quickly, but overlooks the great faults in his own life. In the eye of God there is a great forest tree in your own vision, and but a little speck of dust in your brother's. When you see yourself in the true light, fit only to be nailed to the cross, to be spit upon and scourged, you will never be able to lift up your head again or sit in judgment upon your brother. May God give to all of us the true spirit of humility!

The Spirit of Prejudice

We do not know the names of Arba's other sons, but we will call the second of the Anakim the giant of prejudice. He stands for the spirit of dislike, especially dislikes that are capricious and unreasonable. Many Christian people harbor such feelings, and think they are simply exercising good judgment and discernment of the characters of some of their neighbors. This whole feeling is often built on a misunderstanding. If you knew them as God knows them, you would be ashamed of your misjudgment.

I have seen people who were lifted up out of disease and sin and helped marvelously over the darkest, hardest place in their life, but who almost lost their blessing afterwards through prejudice. Many people have been seriously hindered in their spiritual lives by impressions that after all were false. When they have laid down these impressions and have seen what they really are, and what there is of Christ in other people, they have found their mistake and entered into a fullness of blessing they never before possessed.

If you have a feeling of dislike or prejudice against any of God's dear children, it probably hides the greatest blessing of your life. The dislike is the devil's cloud. Hidden away behind the alienation lies Hebron, the very mountain top from which you may see the King in His beauty and behold the land which is very far off. The people turned from Jesus because He came from Nazareth, asking scornfully, "Nazareth! Can anything good come from there?" (John 1:46). They did not want any blessing which came from that source. You must make up your mind that your great blessings will often come to you from the most forbidding places.

Dislike of eccentric people, perhaps, will hinder your spiritual life, till you lay it down at the feet of Christ. Then the thing you disliked will become a means of great blessing. Put away your malice, prejudice and hatred. You cannot have Jesus in the heart and keep them there too. Become open and frank as a babe toward every child of God. You will find that love is always twice blessed to him that gives and to him that receives.

The Spirit of Pleasure

We will call Arba's third son pleasure, including the love of ease, the love of the world and all other selfish loves. This may have power over us through any thing to which we give our heart. It may be an idol in the household, or love of some dear friend or earthly possessions. Regardless of the size of it, if it gets the heart away from God it is wrong. We are to do the things that please not us but God. We are not to follow our fancy or our choice about things, but say always, "Lord, what will You have me to do?" If we would have His blessing constantly, we must love what He loves, and, indeed, receive our very preferences from Him. Living to please God is the true aim of the holy heart and the true secret of happiness. We are to "live a life worthy of the Lord and . . . please him in every way" (Colossians 1:10). But she "who lives for pleasure is dead even while she lives" (1 Timothy 5:6).

The capture of Hebron suggests these four forms of evil in the heart that are antagonistic to the life of God in the soul. They are self-will, pride, prejudice and pleasure. When these are cast out, the soul can live the life of love and consecration. Then we will walk constantly in the light of His love. Jesus said, "[The Father] has not left me alone, for I always do what pleases him" (John 8:29). This is Hebron.

The Wisdom of the Flesh

The second choice inheritance was Kiriath Sepher, which was taken by Othniel. We have already seen that this was the City of Books, and it teaches us that the wisdom of the flesh is of no value in God's sight. Hebron, however, was captured first. There can be no great spiritual light till love has come. We do not want much freight for the head until the heart has been ballasted. A ship will flounder if it is top-heavy, and so will a Christian. Get the heart filled first, then will come all the illumination from the Holy Spirit that is needed.

There are two sides to this subject. First, the old library must be burned; then God's light can come in. Are you willing to part with your old books?

The traditions of men is one category of books. These include your old ideas, maxims and traditions, the things that have been handed down for centuries. As the fathers thought and lived, so do the children. There are books full of superstitious nonsense, signs, ill omens, and all such satanic shadows. God would have you go straight against the whole of these silly lies. Burn up all these natural books, and take God's thoughts instead.

There are also books full of your own natural reason. They teach you to walk by your common sense and exercise your own clear-headed judgment about things. They do not tell you to look to the Holy Spirit for guidance. You may think it uncalled for to turn away from these things. But God says, "Trust in the LORD with all your heart and lean not on your own understanding" (Proverbs 3:5).

The library contains books on theology, written by good men. They are full of man's reasonings about the Bible, and they ask you to believe based only on the certificate of one of their doctorates. Take no man's leadership apart from God's Word. The wisest and best theologians disagree on almost every department of truth. There must be something wrong somewhere. Take God's Word only. Truth is not fivefold or twofold. It is onefold. Do not lean too strongly on the wisdom of any man.

But it is not enough to burn the old library of Kiriath Sepher. We want a new one. And God has it for us. There is, first, His precious Word of Truth with its inexhaustible fullness. Deeper and deeper will we now fathom its glorious teachings and receive the unfolding of its light as we dwell in the land of promise. There is no interpreter of Scripture like a spiritual experience. How it glows with light and glory when we can trace it in the echo of all our most sacred, inward experiences! And above all other teachers the heavenly Comforter leads us into all truth.

How precious is the Bible to a holy, consecrated heart! How its pages glow with light and love and transcribe themselves upon the memory and the soul! What a choice possession has it become to many a land of Light and Truth, flowing with milk and honey indeed! "They are more precious than gold. . . . They are sweeter than honey, than honey from the comb" (Psalm 19:10).

But there are other books in this blessed city. There is the light of personal revelation through the Holy Spirit. He would indeed be poorly honoring the written Word who denied the reality of the Living Word. The Holy Spirit reveals light through the law written in the heart, the voice of the Shepherd, the light of His face, and the inward communications of the Comforter Himself directly to the heart. The Holy Spirit guides, comforts, commands, and suggests through impulses, thoughts and feelings, devotion, praise, prayer or holy gladness as He is pleased to impart. From Hebron, the place of love, God waits to lead us over to Kiriath Sepher, the place of heavenly light and unerring guidance.

The Springs

There is a beautiful story connected with Acsah in this account. When Othniel won Kiriath Sepher, Caleb gave him his daughter Acsah for his wife. She then claimed and received from her father springs of water, and he gave her the upper and the lower springs.

What are the upper springs? They surely are typical of those things in the divine life that touch the higher parts of our being, the spiritual elements in the soul. The divine life within us should be a spring flowing spontaneously, like water from an artesian well. The springs of prayer should flow responsively to the sweet movings of His Spirit within you. There are springs of joy that must not be clogged for a moment. Never be despondent because everything around is forbidding. Your joy is heavenly joy.

Achash received also the lower springs. They typify the blessings of temporal life—the grace we need in our earthly spheres.

First, there are the springs of health for the body. He has promised that "their health will spring forth speedily" (Isaiah 58:8, KJV). When His physical life becomes a part of ours the feet are ready to fly, the hands become strong for daily work, and the whole system receives new vigor and energy.

Then there are springs of joy and blessing which God lets down into the common experiences of everyday life, which to most of you is one of toil. Blessed be God, all labor can be done in gladness. God is able and willing to meet you there and fill you with freshness and joy in the midst of all your work, so that life will be full of zest no matter what the occupation.

The springs of joy need not be disturbed by the variety of the vessels into which they pour. The joy is not in yourself or your calling at all. The joy is in the heart, because God is there and nothing can disturb it. You may come in contact with painful, grieving, disheartening things, but the joy will be undisturbed. Learn to pray the prayer of Jabez, "Keep me from harm so that I will be free from pain" (1 Chronicles 4:10). Then you will go forth with a coat of mail. The places where you walk may smell of brimstone and fire, but your shoes are of iron and brass and you will walk safely through them. The air may be thick around you with the fumes of hell, but you will be safe, for you are breathing the upper air, and while that lasts you need fear no evil.

Have you taken Hebron? Have you won Kiriath Sepher? Do you have Acsah's heritage, a south land bending to the hot sun, dry and scorched for want of water, but divinely irrigated by the upper and the nether springs? If Jesus is with you in that land it will be turned into a paradise. Wells of living water will be there, and it will blossom like a heavenly garden. Let the water in. Let God come into your heart, and the artesian springs will flow forth abundantly.

Many have little to fill their hearts and lives, but if you have God you can go forth claiming victory.

I ask Thee for the daily strength,
    To none that ask denied,
A mind to blend with outward things
    While keeping at Thy side.
Content to fill a little place
    If Thou be glorified.

There are briers besetting every path
    That call for patient care;
There is a crook in every lot,
    And a constant seed for prayer;
But a loving heart that leans on Thee
    Is happy anywhere.

CHAPTER 8

Lessons about Service

Therefore, since we are receiving a kingdom that cannot be shaken, let us be thankful, and so worship God acceptably with reverence and awe. (Hebrews 12:28)

The book of Joshua teaches many choice lessons respecting Christian service as one of the elements in a consecrated life. Joshua himself is introduced to us, in the earlier notices of his history, as Moses' servant. He had to learn to serve before he could command. Moses also is called the servant of the Lord. Joshua, however, stands as the type of a higher service, inasmuch as the service of the gospel is higher than that of the law. And in the life of full consecration our service for Christ is freer, nobler and more effectual than we can ever know in the wilderness.

Entire Consecration

The first lesson we learn from this book of object lessons is that it is impossible to do much service for God without ourselves fully entering into the experience of entire consecration. We have a striking illustration of this in the case of the two tribes of Reuben and Gad and the half tribe of Manasseh, who chose their inheritance on the wilderness side of Jordan, leaving their families there and afterwards returning themselves. But who, at the same time, shared the struggle of their brethren and fought the battles of the Lord through all the years of the conquest.

They seem to be the types of the many Christians who choose their inheritance on the borders of the world. These Christians are not wholly separated themselves, still less in their families and possessions, from the world, by the dividing line of a real experience of death. Many of whom, at the same time, do much real service for the cause of Christ and for the help of others. Like these three tribes they have visited the land of promise and can tell you very much about it. They have even helped to lead many others into it, and have fought nobly for the testimony of God concerning full salvation and for His cause in every way. But this good land is not their personal and permanent home.

They will frankly confess that they do not live there in the fullest sense, and that to them this higher teaching is a beautiful theory. Indeed, they do not altogether desire to make it their exclusive abode. They prefer the pastures on the plains of Gilead and the rich possessions on the earth side of Jordan. They do not think it best to require their families to go through the sacrifices, self-denials and privations that would be required in crossing the Jordan. Their short-sighted vision does not perceive the future trials that will come from their worldly foes on the battleground of coming ages, when their beautiful estates will be trodden by the feet of Assyrian and Babylonian conquerors, their lovely homes desolated by heathen foes, or themselves enticed into forbidden alliances with the sons and daughters of an idolatrous and godless world.

Thousands of professing Christians are living in just such circumstances and being blighted by such influences. And yet the husbands and fathers and even the mothers and sisters of many such homes are doing much earnest work for Christ, and fighting many of the battles of the Lord. Joshua recognized the services of Reuben and Gad, gave them their full share in the spoils of victory, and sent them back with honorable appreciation, reward and blessing.

And so, still, God accepts the services of many of His children, who are like them, and rewards them as far as He can. Yet He sees how sad and foolish is their choice, and how much higher the blessing and reward of a wholly consecrated life. Let us not only visit the land of promise, but let us choose it as our inheritance. Let us live in it ourselves and stay there, and let us not only enter it for ourselves, but let us never rest until those we love have their full and permanent inheritance within its safe and happy confines.

There is no place so dangerous as the borders of the world and the threshold of the kingdom. The borderland is always Satan's very battleground and the Christian's place of extremest peril. It is possible to sail so close to the whirlpool as to be sucked into the vortex; so near to the burning breath of the pit that our sails will be scorched and consumed by the fiery winds and we left helpless to return.

In contrast with the two and a half tribes referred to, we have in Joshua the beautiful picture of the inheritance of the Levites in their 48 cities, distributed throughout all parts of the land. The Levites stand as the special types of service, a service that springs from separation and entire dedication to God. Selected as the substitutes of Israel's firstborn, they represented, emphatically, the idea of redemption. They were separated from all earthly aims by the fact that they possessed no distinct inheritance or land. The Lord Himself was their inheritance, and the choicest cities of all the tribes were assigned to them as their permanent homes. They were specially fitted to emphasize the truth that true separation to God and a really consecrated life brings us into the possession of all things in Him.

There was not a district of Canaan where the Levites did not have the choicest cities. There was not a tribe that they did not share, in some sense, in its inheritance, and in return, diffused among it the hallowed influence of their presence, example and service. They were the teachers of the nation and the leaders of all true service for God. Their distribution and inheritance teach us that God wants the principle of entire consecration exemplified in every part of our Christian life. Therefore, He sent the Levites through every part of Canaan and located them among all the tribes of Israel that there might be no region where this supreme thought of dedication to Himself would not be constantly set forth in their example. And so He wants the spirit of the Levites manifested in every part of our Christian life. Not only in our temple service, but in our secular callings and domestic enjoyments and affections—from the Dan to the Beersheba of our entire existence.

The principle of true separation to God will bring to us the largest inheritance. Like the Levites, we will not have one portion only, but will possess the whole land in its choicest cities. We will enter into all that is precious, even in the experience of others and the fellowship of God's elect. Of such a soul it is indeed true. "All things are yours, whether Paul or Apollos or Cephas or the world or life or death or the present or the future" (1 Corinthians 3:21-22). And the reason is not that Christ is yours, but that in the true spirit of Levitical consecration "you are of Christ, and Christ is of God" (3:23).

Every Part of Life

Closely related to this is the truth that we can serve God in every part of our life and in every situation where He may place us in His providence. The Levites not only ministered in the tabernacle at Shiloh but in the remotest cities of Canaan. And so the most commonplace occupation, the most secular calling, the most trifling act of earthly duty may involve the highest ministry for Christ.

The oxgoad of Shamgar or the needle of Dorcas are as sacred as the harp of David, the tongue of Paul, and the blood of Stephen. When James the Apostle died, the church could spare even him. But when Dorcas was taken away her place could not be supplied, and she was raised from the dead. It is the glory of the sun that it can illuminate a crumb of broken glass until it shines like costly gems. And it is the highest testimony to Christ when we can reflect His image from the most trivial and commonplace things of our daily life.

Therefore, the chapter that summons to the highest consecration, Romans 12, immediately descends with us into the arena of our common life and adds, "Never be lacking in zeal, but keep your spiritual fervor, serving the Lord" (Romans 12:11). "Do not be proud, but be willing to associate with people of low position" (12:16). "Bless those who persecute you; . . . mourn with those who mourn" (12:14–15).

The highest recompense and the choicest possessions are to be won by brave and faithful service. And he who would attain to the highest place may have all that he will dare to claim and occupy.

This lesson is finely brought out in the account of the two tribes of Ephraim and Manasseh in Joshua 17:14-18. After they had received their inheritance they came to Joshua and claimed, on account of their preeminence among the tribes of Israel as the family of Joseph, that they should receive a special and double inheritance. "Why have you given us only one allotment and one portion?" they ask. "We are a numerous people and the LORD has blessed us abundantly." (Joshua 17:14).

The reply of Joshua is particularly fine. He does not dispute their claim or preeminence. But he demands that they make it good by some proof of their prowess. Then he promises that they can have whatever additional territory they can conquer from the foe. "If you are so numerous . . . and if the hill country of Ephraim is too small for you, go up into the forest and clear land for yourselves there in the land of the Perizzites and Rephaites" (17:15). Then, as they take him at his word, he adds, "You are numerous and very powerful. You will have not only one allotment but the forested hill country as well. Clear it, and its farthest limits will be yours; though the Canaanites have iron chariots and though they are strong, you can drive them out" (17:17-18).

This is still God's message to those who are dissatisfied with their limited sphere, and who are tempted to talk of their special gifts and qualifications for higher service if a better opportunity were afforded them. For all such there is ample room in this great world of sin and sorrow. If they do not have opportunities made ready to the hand, they have but to make them by going out into the ranks of evil and conquering for themselves as large an inheritance of service and blessing as their faith and love can claim. Great souls prove their greatness by making opportunities where others have only complaints. True power will turn the most formidable difficulty into an occasion of victory, and take the boldest adversary prisoner and make him fight in its own ranks.

Joseph's greatness grew out of his prison cell. Had he not been truly great as a slave, he would never have been as a prince. Paul found as good a pulpit when chained to his keeper in a Roman dungeon, or going as a prisoner on shipboard to Rome, as when standing before Agrippa or preaching among his friends at Troas. It is as impossible for true spiritual power to be lost for lack of opportunity as it is to stop the sun from shining or the fountain from flowing. True life and force must find an outlet, and God proves His princes to be of royal birth just where He finds them before He gives them their crowns.

All around us there are ample fields for the exhibition of the noblest Christian heroism and the proving of all the fullness of Christ's grace and power. For each of us there is ample room among the wooded heights and iron chariots of our difficult surroundings for brave endeavors and holy triumphs that will thrill the pulses of heaven and crown us with the unfading glory of Christian heroes. And just as the hardest rocks of earth are the hiding places of the veins of gold and the most costly gems, so we will find that the most difficult and unpromising situations, like the ancient forests of Beth Shan, contain the very soil out of which will grow the most precious fruits of our service and reward.

To be the instrument in God's hands of reclaiming for Christ some utterly wretched and ruined life, or transforming a poor street-waif into a Robert Morrison, or a wretched African captive into the apostle of the Niger, to change some godless neighborhood or some benighted heathen region into a moral paradise, and to wring from the very grasp of difficulty and failure the triumph of truth and righteousness when it seemed like a forlorn hope—surely, this is a higher nobility. It will win a grander prize than to wait in easy indolence for opportunities that cost no effort, or even to fill with reasonable fidelity some place of influence where every circumstance is favorable to success, and faith and courage have little occasion for heroic daring or enduring.

Let us, then, not look so often for promising opportunities as we find them in the very midst of our present situation and in the very bosom of our most formidable difficulties.

It is the property of water to run to the lowest depths and to find its way to the deepest channels. Like its beautiful earthly type, the living water runs downward. The more of divine grace there is in any heart, the more will it prompt its possessor, like the Son of Man, to seek and save the lost.

In Contact with the Deepest Need

The highest Christian life should ever be found in contact with the lowest sinfulness and the deep-

est need. Those who have become too high in
Christian attainment to feel called to work for sinners, have probably become too high for the companionship of the Good Shepherd. The more of
His spirit we cherish, and the more of His likeness
we possess, the more will we be found, like Him,
in the midst of publicans and sinners, seeking if,
by any means, we may save some.

All this is finely set forth in the book of Joshua.
Almost the first picture, in that beautiful manual
of the higher Christian life, is the story of the salvation of poor Rahab, the harlot of Jericho. Her
condition was, undoubtedly, one of great wicked-
ness and deep degradation. The Canaanite nations
were infamous for the most unnatural and abominable depravity, and she was, probably, a true
type of the most abandoned of her race and her
sex.

But when the messengers of Israel came to her
doors she received them kindly, believed their tid-
ings, and earnestly asked for their protection when
the hour of her country's ruin should have come.
They gave her a simple token by which her home
could be recognized—a crimson cord suspended
from her window. This suggested, if not typified,
the blood of Calvary, through which still the sinful soul is saved. It promised her that the token
would be respected in the hour of danger, and all
who took refuge under it be saved.

When that hour came Jericho fell with a crash of
doom and a shriek of terror. Amid all the confusion
of that awful day—the falling walls, the shout of Is-

rael's camp, the cries and shrieks from the doomed city, the groans of the dying inhabitants, and the wild excitement of the victorious army rushing in and destroying all before them—that crimson token was not forgotten. That little section of the walls of Jericho with its scarlet banner flying from the ramparts remained unshaken, and every soldier of the Hebrew camp respected the signal and spared the woman and all her household.

This picture was a beautiful foreshadowing of the coming gospel and the great redemption through the blood of Christ, proclaiming to the most lost and vile, eternal security from the judgment of God for all who put their trust in the cross of Calvary and the atoning blood. It was a beautiful lesson, too, to the consecrated hosts of God, that amid all the victories of faith and all the higher attainments of the land of promise, they are not to forget as one of their chief concerns, the sinful and the lost, and the blessed and heavenly work of winning them to Jesus and sheltering them beneath His cross.

Not only was Rahab saved from destruction, but she was received into the very household of Israel and became one of the most honored names in the very ancestry of their kings—and still more, of the very Redeemer Himself. For, when we come to trace the genealogy of the Son of Man, according to the flesh, we find in His wondrous pedigree, not only the illustrious names of David and Abraham, but also, Ruth the Moabitess, and Rahab the harlot.

God is still calling the princes of His kingdom from the very ranks of deepest degradation, saying to the sons and daughters of sin and shame, "This is my brother, my sister, and my mother." He is always waiting to raise the most helpless of our fallen race to that glorious company who will yet shine like a cloud of splendor around the throne of heaven. Of these, admiring angels will be asked, "These in white robes—who are they, and where did they come from?" And the answer will be, "These are they who have come out of the great tribulation; they have washed their robes and made them white in the blood of the Lamb" (Revelation 7:13-14).

The Sinner's Refuge

The same beautiful lesson is taught still more emphatically in the closing incidents of the book of Joshua. While it opens with the story of Rahab, it concludes with the appointment of the cities of refuge, teaching the same lesson in a still more vivid and glorious manner.

These six cities were set apart in all sections of the land of Canaan as places of refuge for the manslayer when pursued by the Goel, or avenger of blood. They were within easy approach of every part of the land. Public roads were provided leading directly to them, kept constantly open and in good repair at the expense of the government. Every torrent was bridged and every obstacle removed. And wherever the crossroads might render the way uncertain, finger-posts were erected, opening to the refuge and preventing all possible mistake. Ample provision was made within the city for the supply of all the wants of the fugitive. The gates were always open, and no weapon was permitted within the inclosure. There the unhappy man could rest in perfect safety until his case was formally adjudicated upon or until the death of the high priest, when he was free to return to his home in perfect safety, and no one dared molest him. This was not a refuge for willful murderers, but for those who had unintentionally committed manslaughter.

This merciful provision was a significant type of Jesus Christ as the sinner's refuge. He is not the refuge for those who desire to continue in sin, or sinfully reject or disobey Him. But for the abandoned soul that is willing to leave his sin and turn to Him, His mercy is ever open and free. Like the ancient refuge, He is near to the most hopeless and helpless. The way to His feet is ever open and close at hand. There are no barriers across the path. "Whoever will may come," and find an instant and gracious welcome and ample provision for all his future need. Not only so, but His own death as our great High Priest has settled all claims against us, and given us a full and eternal freedom from all the charges of the law and the judgment of God on account of our sin.

The very names of these ancient cities were suggestive of the fullness of Christ's provision. Kadesh, the first on the west of the Jordan, signifies "righteousness." It suggests the provision we find in Christ for our complete justification and cleansing. Shechem, the second on the west, literally means "a shoulder." It represents the Almighty strength that Christ supplies to the helpless sinner, and with which He upholds our weakness and carries all our needs and burdens. Hebron, the third of these cities, means "friendship" and "fellowship." It tells of the love and communion into which we come when we receive Jesus. We are not only justified, sanctified and strengthened, but we are loved even as He is loved. We enter into His perfect fellowship and everlasting friendship, finding also in Him the high and holy companionship of His people, and the intimacies and mutual bonds and blessings of the household of faith.

Crossing to the east of the Jordan we first come to Bozrah, whose name signifies "security." It signifies the eternal security into which Christ receives His trusting children. He is bound to them by His covenant and oath, and declares, "I give them eternal life, and they shall never perish; no one can snatch them out of my hand" (John 10:28).

Ramoth midway on the eastern side of Jordan, means "lofty." It typifies the exalted place of privilege, honor, blessing and progress to which Christ receives us. He lifts us up from our degradation, exalts us to share His rights and glories, and calls us on from strength to strength, and from grace to glory. "God raised us up with Christ and seated us with him in the heavenly realms in Christ Jesus" (Ephesians 2:6).

The last of the cities of refuge, Golan, means "a circle." It represents the completeness and eternity of our redemption in Christ. All these together present the sublime picture of the fullness of Jesus as the refuge of the unworthy and the lost. And such a chain of living monuments of the divine mercy in all parts of the land could not fail to afford the most emphatic and continual witness to the gospel of the coming redemption.

So, in our land of promise, there should be the constant witness of Christ as a Savior, held up so vividly and so universally that men never can lose sight of it. Holiness so cold and inaccessible causes poor sinners to feel that it is too high for their attainment and too hard for their helplessness to reach. But the gospel holds out to all classes and conditions of sinful men the constant proclamation of a Savior, as complete and wonderful as these ancient names set forth.

Christians and Sinners

But the very climax of our lesson is seen in the fact that all these cities of refuge were Levitical cities. They were committed wholly to the administration of that class of Israel's officials whom, as we have seen, God appointed as the special types of entire consecration. It was to the Levites' hands that the sinner was committed. It was the Levite who met him with open arms at the open gate, ushered him into his place of security, and tenderly provided for all his needs. This teaches us, with singular power, that those who are most fully consecrated are the very ones to whom the Master looks to "rescue the perishing, care for the dying," and "snatch them in pity from sin and the grave."

Oh, that every consecrated heart, every circle of professed holiness might be a city of refuge, where poor sinners would know that they would ever find a welcome. This is the service to which Christ is calling His consecrated people. "Lovest thou me?" He still tenderly asks. "Then, feed my lambs, my sheep, and my feeble, wandering ones." Let not only the Spirit, but also the bride say, "Come!" and her tender voice, her beckoning hand, and her gentle face ever seem to echo the inviting call: "Whoever wishes, let him take the free gift of the water of life" (Revelation 22:17).

A Christian lady had become worn in her life-work and longed for rest. One night she dreamed that she was floating up to the gates of heaven on a crystal sea without a ripple of fear. Just before her were the shining gates and she could see already the forms of the blessed and hear the distinct echoes of their harps and songs. Her soul was filled with rapture, the anticipation of eternal rest. Eagerly, she pressed forward to reach the heavenly haven. Suddenly, she heard a cry behind her, and looking back she saw a sinking child struggling amid the waves. She turned to rescue it and instantly it seemed that a cord from her heart strings fell behind her and became a little cable to which the lost one clung as she drew her gently along, feeling at the same time a pang of pain from the pressure of her burden.

A moment later, there was another cry, and she saw a drowning woman calling for her help, and all around her she now beheld the sinking forms of helpless human beings, all looking to her for rescue. She turned her back upon the glorious city, reached out her hands to the struggling ones, and each in turn fastened to her very heart, by the cords of her own life, a burden of living agony and love. But the burden was more blessed than even the glory which she had just been entering. Lifting up her voice to heaven, she cried, "Father, not yet. I ask no more for rest. A little longer let me suffer and toil for these, and bring them with me when I come. The joy of my heaven will be a hundredfold more because of their salvation."

Yes, this is the purpose of our consecration. Not that we may be happy, nor even that we may be fit for service and clothed with heavenly love and power, does the Master call us to a consecrated life in the land of promise. "Therefore, since we are receiving a kingdom that cannot be shaken, let us be thankful, and so worship God acceptably with reverence and awe" (Hebrews 12:28).

> Not now; for I have wanderers in the
> distance,
> And thou must call them in with patient
> love;
> Not now, for I have sheep upon the
> mountains,

And thou must follow them where'er they
rove.

Go with the name of Jesus to the dying,
And speak that Name in all its living
power;
Why should thy fainting heart grow chill
and weary?
Canst thou not watch with Me one little
hour?

One little hour! and then the glorious
crowning,
The golden harp-strings, and the victor's
palm:
One little hour! and then the hallelujah!
Eternity's long, deep, thanksgiving psalm!

CHAPTER 9

Christ Himself Our True Inheritance

I say to myself, "The LORD is my portion;
therefore I will wait for him."
(Lamentations 3:24)

The highest Christian life is not the experience of holiness, or even of the richest gifts and graces of the Holy Spirit, but the life of Christ Himself manifest in our mortal flesh. It is that complete and perfect union with His person expressed by the apostle in the words, "For you died, and your life is now hidden with Christ in God. When Christ, who is your life, appears, then you also will appear with him in glory" (Colossians 3:3-4). And again, in Paul's own personal testimony, "But when God, who set me apart from birth and called me by his grace, was pleased to reveal his Son in me . . . I did not consult any man" (Galatians 1:15-16).

This is the true substance and supreme inheritance of the land of promise. And this is the truth

135

vividly set forth in the book of Joshua. The very name of Joshua is substantially the same as that of Jesus. And that brave and faithful captain was, no doubt, designed to be the type of the Captain of our salvation, whom God has set forth as a Leader and Commander to the people. It is He who brings us into the promised land as Moses never could have done. It is He who becomes our victorious Leader in the good fight of faith. It is He who divides to us our inheritance of spiritual blessing.

The Person of Jesus

There are four passages in this remarkable book which set forth very definitely and strikingly the Person of Jesus.

The very first assurance of God to His servant was His own personal presence. This was to be the antidote to every fear and the ground of every confidence. "No one will be able to stand up against you all the days of your life. As I was with Moses, so I will be with you. . . . Do not be terrified; do not be discouraged, for the LORD your God will be with you wherever you go" (Joshua 1:5, 9). It was for this that Moses had specially pleaded, and refused the presence of the mightiest angel in comparison. "How will anyone know that you are pleased with me and with your people unless you go with us?" (Exodus 33:16). And this became the secret of Joshua's success. Indeed this is the one transcendent promise of both the Old and the New Testaments.

To Abraham, God's great promise was, "Do not be afraid, Abram. I am your shield, your very great reward" (Genesis 15:1). Abraham did not know anything but God. When he was told to go out from his country he went leaving much behind him, but he had God. So Isaac was driven from place to place by the Philistines, but he, too, had always the promise, "I will be with you and will bless you" (26:3).

When Jacob was fleeing, a fugitive from home and land, God appeared to him saying, "I am with you and will watch over you wherever you go, and I will bring you back to this land" (28:15).

When Moses hesitated to undertake the great work God had given him, because of his stammering tongue, the word of the Lord that came to him was, "Certainly I will be with you and with your mouth"(see Exodus 3, 4). He did not promise to make Moses eloquent and He never did, but He promised to be with him and in that power Moses prevailed.

When Balaam looked over the host of Israel, though greatly longing to curse them, he was compelled to recognize the presence of God with them. "The LORD their God is with them; the shout of the King is among them" (Numbers 23:21).

Caleb, when the heart of the people melted because of the false report of the land, earnestly pleaded with them to go up at once and possess it, saying, "We should go up and take possession of the land, for we can certainly do it" (13:30).

Not an idea, a program.
Principal,

David's source of comfort in his great trials was the presence of God. It was not a principle nor an idea of Him who possessed him, but it was the consciousness of One of whom he could say, "Whom have I in heaven but you? And earth has nothing I desire besides you" (Psalm 73:25).

The prophecies of Isaiah are full of the same precious promise. The coming of the Lord Himself among His people was the constant burden of Isaiah's message. "So do not fear, for I am with you; do not be dismayed, for I am your God. I will strengthen you and help you; I will uphold you with my righteous right hand" (Isaiah 41:10).

The prophets of the restoration echo the same message. God spoke to Haggai commanding the people to rebuild the temple. He encouraged them in their work with the simple promise: " 'I am with you,' declares the LORD" (Haggai 1:13). That was all. Months passed away and there came not another whisper even from Him; yet the people went forward with their work. Then He spoke to Haggai the second time, saying, " 'Be strong, all you people of the land,' declares the LORD, 1and work. For I am with you,' declares the LORD Almighty" (2:4).

The Old Testament closes with a glorious prophecy of the immediate appearing of the Lord among His people in bodily form. " 'Then suddenly the Lord you are seeking will come to his temple; the messenger of the covenant, whom you desire, will come,' says the LORD Almighty" (Malachi 3:1).

New Testament Promise

In the New Testament this promise of the divine presence is repeated with new definiteness and fullness. Jesus talks always about Himself. "But take heart! I have overcome the world" (John 16:33). "It is I; don't be afraid" (6:20). "I too will love him and show myself to him" (14:21). "I will not leave you comfortless: I will come to you" (14:18, KJV). "Go and make disciples of all nations. . . . And surely I am with you always, to the very end of the age" (Matthew 28:19-20). He adds also the presence of the Comforter to these promises. "He lives with you and will be in you" (John 14:17). "But the Counselor, the Holy Spirit . . . will teach you all things" (14:26).

There is this difference between the Old and New Testaments on this subject. The Old promises God's presence _with_ His people; the New promises His presence _in_ them. Joshua, Moses and David never said the Lord was in them, but always spoke of His presence with them. It is possible in this dispensation to have the very nature of God put into the soul. We may be as closely united to Him as the branches are to the vine, so that our brain, our heart, our hands and feet, indeed every part of our being will feel the presence of God within us. Christ may be so one with us as to put His life into our entire being and influence our volitions, our choices, our desires, and the very affection of our hearts.

In the book of Revelation Jesus is pictured as standing and knocking at the door of the heart asking His children to let Him in (3:20). His chief complaint against them is that they are satisfied without Him.

This blessed promise of God's presence runs from the beginning to the end of the Bible. It seems as though there were nothing in Revelation but God, or in Christianity but Christ. Christian life is just Christ life. The land of promise is the land where Jesus is revealed in all His fullness.

Joshua's vision was of Christ as a manifested Presence. Just after they had crossed the Jordan, and before their first conflict with Jericho, the Lord Jesus Himself suddenly appeared to Joshua as a mighty soldier with drawn sword across his path. Instantly, the brave warrior demanded, "Are you for us or for our enemies?" (Joshua 5:13). And the answer prostrated him on his face in veneration and worship. "Neither, . . . but as commander of the army of the LORD I have now come" (5:14).

From this time Joshua understood, as never before, that there ever walked before him and beside him a personal Presence, no less than the very Son of God Himself. Joshua was no more to count himself as captain, but to follow his Leader, and to know that where He led it must be victory. He had received the promise of His presence before, but now the Lord came visibly and personally to meet him.

Jacob also chose the covenant blessing and stepped out in faith, leaving the land that he knew was to be his. As he lay down to rest at Bethel, Jehovah met him in the silent night. And after that vision at Bethel His presence was henceforth real to Jacob forevermore.

Has God thus become manifest to you? Has the Holy Spirit made the presence of Christ a living, bright reality to your consciousness? He will reveal Himself to the sincere and seeking heart. You cannot lift up the cry, "I would see Jesus," in vain. The Holy Spirit will make His presence real. Do not be satisfied until you know His appearing.

The Apostle John uses two words with reference to the apprehension of Jesus. He sometimes speaks of believing Him, but he often uses the word "know." Do you know Jesus? Has the Commander of the Lord's army appeared to you? All through the wilderness Joshua had not seen Him. We must enter the land of promise and cross the Jordan before we can see Him.

In California there has been erected upon Mt. Hamilton the most wonderful observatory and telescope in the world. They did not put it down in the valley of San José, but away up on the mountain height where there would be no mists or fogs to obstruct the view. In the clear, transparent light of those upper regions, unclouded views of the celestial world could be obtained. So, dear friend, we must get on the high ground of the land of promise if we would reach the place of heavenly vision. There we will see Jesus. When Abraham was living his life of human contrivance and unbelief, God did not come to him at once. During the years of his connection with Hagar, and while he was trying to help God fulfill His promises, he never had a sight of God. We cannot see Jesus if we are not in the place of simple faith and obedience.

His Victorious Power

The effect of seeing Jesus will be the manifestation of His victorious power. It will put your own self-strength out of the way. The spirit of self is never put away until there has come to the soul this vision of Christ. Joshua was thoroughly dead to every evil thing at this time, but he was still conscious of himself. He was to do the work and fight the battles. But God stepped across his path and said, "No, Joshua, it is not your work at all. I am to be leader and do the planning and fight the battles. You must simply follow Me." Joshua had to take the position of a servant. This changed the position of things altogether. It altered the very center of his life. When we reach this place, things will be put in their true order. The burden will be upon His shoulder, and we will have no care or struggle.

The highest form of spiritual dying is to cease from our own leadership, wisdom, strength and responsibility, and to let the Lord Jesus be made unto us of God, wisdom, righteousness, sanctification, redemption, and all in all. This will prove to us the very secret both of courage and of victory.

Our enemies do not fear us, but before Him none dare to stand. We may have few associates and feeble resources, but if we have the Lord we must prevail. This was the spectacle that filled Balaam with admiration as he gazed on the tents of Israel. "The LORD their God is with them; the shout of the King is among them" (Numbers 23:21). This was the dying shout of Wesley, "The best of all is God is with us."

When the Duke of Wellington had no reinforcements to send to one of his outnumbered battalions, he galloped to the field himself, accompanied by his staff. The hard-pressed veterans, as they saw him, shouted, "Here comes the duke himself, better than a whole brigade." If we could but realize who it is that goes before us in our hardest places, and the myriads of angelic hosts that await His bidding, how little would we fear our strongest foes, and with hope exclaim in triumph in the darkest hour,

> I fear no foe with Thee at hand to bless;
> Earth hath no ills, and tears no bitterness.
> Where is death's sting, where, grave, thy
> victory?
> I triumph still if Thou abide with me.

We have already seen that the Levites had no portion in the division of the land among the tribes, and the reason was that the Lord was their inheritance. If the inheritance of the tribes is expressive of the special gifts and graces of the Spirit, or of the blessings of God's grace and providence, then the special inheritance of the Levites must imply that God Himself is better than any or all of His gifts. Especially is this truth connected with the idea of service, of which the Levites were the expression.

Christ Himself is our strength and wisdom for all the service for which He calls us. He does not require us to supply the resources for our Christian work from our own talents or strength or qualifications, but in absolute dependence upon Himself. He bids the weakest go forth and accept Him to use their helplessness and through His strength make it effectual to the pulling down of strongholds.

Therefore, we read that "God chose [by actual preference] the foolish things of the world to shame the wise; God chose the weak things of the world to shame the strong. He chose the lowly things of this world and the despised things—and the things that are not—to nullify the things that are" (1 Corinthians 1:27-28). He used the rod of Moses to humiliate the pride of Pharaoh, simply because He was behind it. He used the ram horns of Israel to beat down the walls of Jericho, simply because He followed up the faith and obedience of His people. He could not use Gideon's 30,000 until they were reduced to 300—weak enough for God to be in the victory. David's sling was stronger than Goliath's sword because it was used in the name of the Lord. Five barley loaves and two small fishes were sufficient for 5,000 when Jesus blessed them. And so the humblest laborers and the most limited resources have usually been honored of God in the accomplishment of the greatest results in His work. Consecrated faith, humility and earnestness are mightier weapons in the aggressive work of Christianity than human learning and magnificent religious forms.

If we would be true Levites, willing to let the Master use us, we may find in Himself and the indwelling fullness of His Holy Spirit all the resources of faith, wisdom, love and power that our work requires. The baptism of the Holy Spirit includes every quality essential for spiritual power: the faith that claims divine results; the power of prayer, by far the mightiest of spiritual forces; the love which will win the lost; the tact and wisdom that will speak the word in season, or do the fit act in the appropriate time or stand still when God is more glorified by silence than by officiousness.

The history and condition of Christianity today teems with illustrations of the marvelous usefulness which God can give the humblest instrumentalities that are wholly consecrated to the glory of Christ and baptized with His Spirit and fullness.

Timnath Serah is a type of Christ our portion. This word means, literally, the City of the Sun. It may well denote the spiritual inheritance of which Christ Himself is the substance and the glory. "I am the light of the world," the Lord Jesus has said. "Whoever follows me will never walk in darkness, but will have the light of life" (John 8:12) "If we walk in the light, as he is in the light, we have fellowship with one another, and the blood of Jesus, his Son, purifies us from all sin" (1 John 1:7-9). This is the city of the sun—the life of intimate and unclouded fellowship with the Lord Jesus Christ. Glorious things are spoken of this city of God.

It is an abode of delightful happiness. "Blessed are those who have learned to acclaim you, who walk in the light of your presence, O Lord. They rejoice in your name all day long" (Psalm 89:15-16). "For with you is the fountain of life; in your light we see light" (36:9). "You will fill me with joy in your presence, with eternal pleasures at your right hand" (16:11).

It is a place of abundant grace. "For the Lord God is a sun and shield; the Lord bestows favor and honor; no good thing does he withhold from those whose walk is blameless" (84:11). Here are found, as in some sunny land of boundless fruitage and luxuriance, all the rich and abundant fruits of the Tree of Life. Grace so rich and full that it sometimes rises even to the heights of glory; as through the rent veil the brightness of the inner chamber streams around us, even in the earthly sanctuary. They who dwell in this happy city have all things that divine love and wisdom can bestow.

"No good thing does he withhold from those whose walk is blameless." "My God will meet all your needs according to his glorious riches in Christ Jesus" (Philippians 4:19). This is not only the riches of grace, but He draws even upon the reserve fund laid by in heaven and grants according to the riches of His glory. For Jesus said, "I have given them the glory that you gave me" (John 17:22).

They who dwell in the city of the sun enjoy the constant manifestation of the presence of Jesus. The King is among them and His presence is constantly manifested, for He has said, "Whoever has my commands and obeys them, . . . I too will love him and show myself to him" (14:21). This literally means, "I will shine forth gloriously" to him.

The city of the sun is a place of healing, and they who dwell in this favored abode enjoy immunity from the over-mastering physical evils of life. "But for you who revere my name, the sun of righteousness will rise with healing in its wings. And you will go out and leap like calves released from the stall" (Malachi 4:2). Even physical light is healing, but the light of Jesus and the life of Jesus are the very strength of our physical vitality. They who abide with Him "will renew their strength. They will soar on wings like eagles; they will run and not grow weary, they will walk and not be faint" (Isaiah 40:31).

The city of the sun is a place of delightful guidance. "Whoever follows me will never walk in darkness, but will have the light of life" (John 8:12). They who thus abide with Christ have the delightful sense of His constant direction and walk in His personal guidance, in the sound of His voice and in the print of His footsteps.

There is an abode of unclouded and everlasting light and blessedness. "Your sun will never set

again, and your moon will wane no more; the
LORD will be your everlasting light, and your days
of sorrow will end" (Isaiah 60:20). True, they are
not free from the trials and temptations of earth,
but they have learned the secret of rising above
them and dwelling in the light of a higher sphere.

There is an altitude where no cloud can reach us
and no mist obscure our everlasting sunshine. And
for those who have risen with Christ, "The path of
life leads upward for the wise to keep him from going down to the grave" (Proverbs 15:24). The sor-
rows are still there, but we are looking at them from
the throne, where we already sit with our victorious
Christ. There is a fellowship with Jesus even on
earth that need never be interrupted; a sunlight that
need never be withdrawn; a peace that need never
be broken by a ripple of unrest. And there are souls
on earth that walk in everlasting light. Their feet
tread the troubled waves; their forms often are lost
to sight amid the clouds that encompass them. But
their heads are ever in the unclouded light of the everlasting sunshine.

Have we entered into this delightful abode?
Have we claimed our citizenship in Timnath
Serah? Can we sing with the psalmist, "The LORD
is my light and my salvation—whom shall I fear?
The LORD is the stronghold of my life—of whom
shall I be afraid" (Psalm 27:1)?

Our All in God

The only secret of it is, to seek and find our all
in God. Joshua's inheritance may have had noth-

ing else, but it had infinite sunshine. The land may have been small, but he had the sun, the whole sun, the sun in unclouded and unceasing effulgence and glory. When we are satisfied with the smiles of His face, the light of His love, and do not look as much to our surroundings or even to our spiritual emotions and conditions as to His unceasing presence, we, too, will find that life has risen above its most trying variations. We will find that we have reached a country which might also be called, like the strange day of northern Norway, "The Land of the Midnight Sun."

I have seen Christians who were living in the land of the midnight sun, tranquil and happy in the light of Him who was more to them than their surroundings. They are like the martyr Cyprian, who, when asked to recant or his fortune would be taken from him, replied, "You cannot do that, for my treasure is laid up in heaven." When he was threatened with separation from all his friends, the noble hero replied, "You cannot do that either, for my affections are placed on things above where Christ sitteth at the right hand of God." "Then," replied his persecutors, "we will take your life." Cyprian answered, "That, too, is beyond your reach, for I am dead and my life is hid with Christ in God."

Let us get into the city that is above the clouds and the land whose sun no more goes down, and the song that echoes the loudest in the night of sorrow will be our refrain.

I've found a joy in sorrow,
    A secret balm for pain,
A beautiful tomorrow
    Of sunshine after rain.

I've found a branch for healing,
    Near every bitter spring,
A whispered promise stealing
    O'er every broken string.

I've found a glad hosanna
    For every woe and wail,
A handful of sweet manna
    When grapes of Eschol fail.

I've found the Rock of Ages,
    When desert wells are dry;
And after weary stages,
    I've found an Elim nigh.

An Elim with its coolness,
    Its fountains and its shade;
A blessing in its fullness,
    When buds of promise fade.

O'er tears of soft contrition
    I've seen a rainbow light;
A glory and fruition.
    So near! yet out of sight.

'Tis Jesus, my portion forever,
    'Tis Jesus, the First and the Last,

A help very present in trouble.
A shelter from every blast.

To those who set their hearts thus supremely on Him, He reveals, in all its fullness, the light and glory of His presence. And can we look even at the material sun with its dazzling glory, and realize that God has filled it with its fire, and kept it burning and shining for many thousand years, and not feel that He who did so much for a mere material ball will do far more for the soul that Christ redeemed and into which He has actually come to dwell?

Let us open all the windows of our being and receive Him with that confidence which is the condition of His manifested love and presence. And receiving Him with a surrendered and trusting heart, let us go forth to walk in His light, and so shine, in His reflected glory, that others will see our good works and glorify our Father which is in heaven.

The gospel which the world needs most is not a new creed, but a new life; not new truths, but new and living realities; not better ideas, but more strength to fulfill them. The only way to make this real to the men around us is to live it. Yet, not so to live it that they will see our character, but rather so that they will see Christ behind us and reflected through us, in so definite and personal a manner that it will become to them also a possibility for their discouraged and failing lives. Merely to see our excellencies might only discourage them by the contrast with themselves, but to see behind us, as the inspiration and support of all our victories, the real and all-sufficient presence of One who is just as willing to become for them the source of strength and constant health. To hear us say, "I am conscious of being as weak and helpless as my brethren, and yet I can do all things through Christ who strengthens me," this is indeed a living gospel and will lead them to hunger and thirst until they find their rest and satisfaction in Jesus for themselves.

God does not want temples of stone, or even of gold, from which to reflect His glory. But, like the ancient prince in the oriental fable who built a temple for the sun, He wants His sanctuary of transparent glass so that He can shine into every part. Our glory is that we ourselves are invisible. And our only mission is to receive, transmit and reflect the light of His glory and grace. Thus, each of us can be in ourselves a Timnath Serah, and as the world beholds us, it will say, "Come, . . . let us walk in the light of the LORD" (Isaiah 2:5).

Have you this blessed presence? You cannot seek it in vain. He who cannot lie has said, "I will not leave you comfortless: I will come to you" (John 14:18, KJV). Claim the promise with a persistent faith that, like wrestling Jacob, will not let Him go except He bless you.

It is said that one of the Scottish pastors of covenanting times was slow in coming to his pulpit one day, and the sexton was sent to the vestry to enquire. He returned, saying, "I fear he winna come the day, for I aye heard him speakin' to One and saying he wadna come withoot Him. And when I left the other hadna spoken a word, and so I fear he willna come this morn." Yes, that is the way these men were mighty through God to the pulling down of strongholds.

Still, as at Emmaus, He often makes as though He would pass by. But let us constrain Him. He only waits your whole soul's invitation. Let Him in. He is the land of promise. He is the Sun of Timnath Serah. He is the Light and Glory of the city that has no need of the sun.

> Christ to trust and Christ to know
>   Constitute our bliss below;
> Christ to see and Christ to love
>   Constitute our bliss above.

CHAPTER 10

The Danger of Declension

"But my righteous one will live by faith.
And if he shrinks back,
    I will not be pleased with him."

But we are not of those who shrink back and are
destroyed, but of those who believe and are saved.
(Hebrews 10:38-39)

See to it, brothers, that none of you has a sin-
ful, unbelieving heart that turns away from the
living God. (3:12)

The people served the LORD throughout the life-
time of Joshua and of the elders who outlived
him and who had seen all the great things the
LORD had done for Israel. . . .
    After that whole generation had been gath-
ered to their fathers, another generation grew
up, who knew neither the LORD nor what he had
done for Israel. Then the Israelites did evil in the
eyes of the LORD and served the Baals. They for-
sook the LORD, the God of their fathers, who had

> *brought them out of Egypt. They followed and*
> *worshiped various gods of the peoples around*
> *them. They provoked the* LORD *to anger. . . . In*
> *his anger against Israel the* LORD *handed them*
> *over to raiders who plundered them. He sold*
> *them to their enemies all around, whom they*
> *were no longer able to resist. (Judges 2:7-14)*

Such is the sad story of Israel's declension. It is all the more sad because it follows the wonders and triumphs of the book of Joshua. It is far more sad even than the earlier record of their failure in the book of Numbers.

Israel's unbelief in the wilderness was not so aggravated, nor so long and bitter in its effects, as Israel's declension after entering the land of promise. The first arrested their progress for a generation, but the second plunged them for four hundred years into bondage, misery and shame. And so there is often a backsliding in Christian life after conversion and before entire consecration, that leads to much loss and sorrow, and retards the progress of the soul, often for many years.

An Inexcusable Backsliding

But there is another backsliding, after the experience of consecration and the baptism of the Holy Spirit, which is far more inexcusable, and leads to more terrible consequences. It would seem to be against this that the warnings of the epistle to the Hebrews are specially directed. The teaching of the book of Joshua, and especially of the book of

Judges, seems to make it certain that such a declension is indeed possible.

This backsliding for the people of Israel came after incredible triumphs. It came after all the divine manifestations of Joshua's life and leadership, after all the victories of Jericho, Beth Horon and Merom, after all the kings of Canaan had been subdued and their land divided into Israel's inheritance. Even after Joshua's parting charges at Shechem, it came. Israel went back, in the third generation, into idolatry and sin. They forsook the covenant of their God. As a result Israel became subject to the tribes that they had formerly subdued. They were overrun by foreign invaders, and were placed under tribute to all the surrounding nations. They were reduced to a condition of such pitiful humiliation and helplessness that, in the days of Saul, they were not even permitted to have a grindstone to sharpen their very ploughshares, lest it should be used to sharpen their swords for war. The book of Judges is a melancholy picture of their degradation and near apostasy.

A picture as sad, and almost perfectly parallel, can be found in the story of primitive Christianity. The apostolic age of the Church was marked by faith as bold, obedience as implicit, and victory as splendid as the conquest of Joshua. But, alas, before the third generation had come, the spirit of declension had already appeared and another and darker period of idolatry in the very Church of God. Conformity to the spirit of the world and humiliating failure in the conflict with sin and Satan filled up more than three times four hundred years of the dark ages of medieval Christianity, until the very Church seemed to have become apostate. Like Deborah, Barak, Gideon, Samson and Jephthah, only a little remnant of faithful ones could be found here and there in the whole Christian world.

And, in like manner, it is to be feared that there are many examples in individual Christian lives. Many have promising beginnings in the life of consecration, are sealed by the most real and glorious manifestations of the divine presence, grace and power. But these beginnings have afterwards been followed, through lack of vigilance and holy obedience, by gross error, spiritual declension, soul-deceiving sin, and even open disobedience, worldliness, weakness, and what seemed to threaten even final apostasy.

Thanks to the infinite mercy of God, the resources of God's grace and discipline are sufficient for the restoration of even such a soul. But the danger is not less real or the warning less solemn and emphatic. Therefore, we find the New Testament epistles, where they speak of the very highest possibilities of Christian experience, most urgently warning the believer against the danger of backsliding, calling us to ceaseless vigilance and constant obedience. Even where God's eternal faithfulness is most severely pledged to keep us, we are called upon all the more to exercise a spirit of watchfulness and constant dependence on His all-sufficient grace.

Hence, we find John saying in one breath, "The anointing you received from him remains in you" (1 John 2:27). And yet, in the next, "And now, dear children, continue in him" (2:28). We find Jude pointing us "to him who is able to keep [us] from falling," and yet enjoining us to keep ourselves "in God's love as you wait for the mercy of our Lord Jesus Christ to bring you to eternal life" (Jude 24, 21).

We find Peter saying, "The Lord knows how to rescue godly men from trials" (2 Peter 2:9); but adding in the same epistle, "dear friends, . . . be on your guard so that you may not be carried away by the error of lawless men and fall from your secure position" (3:17). He again assures us that "His divine power has given us everything we need for life and godliness" (1:3), but also charges us to be diligent, to make our calling and election sure, for if we do these things, we shall never fall.

We find in chapters 5 and 6 of Hebrews the most solemn parallel of all. Flashing before us is a terrific picture of a soul once enlightened and tasting of the heavenly gift, and then becoming so apostate as to put the Son of God to an open shame. The writer adds immediately, "Even though we speak like this, dear friends, we are confident of better things in your case—things that accompany salvation" (6:9). Then he adds, to keep the balance of hope and fear perfectly adjusted, "We want each of you to show this same diligence to the very end, in order to make your hope sure" (6:11).

So again, in the 10th chapter, the fearful picture of the soul that has "trampled the Son of God under foot, who has treated as an unholy thing the blood of the covenant that sanctified him, and who has insulted the Spirit of grace," is accompanied by the warning, "If he shrinks back, I will not be pleased with him" (10:29, 38). But the gracious encouragement is then added, "But we are not of those who shrink back and are destroyed, but of those who believe and are saved" (10:39).

The same striking antithesis of warning and promise runs throughout Paul's epistles. His letter to the Ephesians lifts us up to the heavenly places, but it also looks down into the deep gulf below and warns us, as no other epistle against the real danger of ungodliness, uncleanliness, untruthfulness, dishonesty, sinful anger, strife, covetousness, drunkenness, and all the wiles of the devil.

And while Paul can exclaim, in the language of the sublimest confidence, "I know whom I have believed, and am convinced that he is able to guard what I have entrusted to him for that day" (2 Timothy 1:12); yet, he also charges Timothy in the same epistle, "Guard the good deposit that was entrusted to you—guard it with the help of the Holy Spirit who lives in us" (1:14). "But you, keep your head in all situations, endure hardship, do the work of an evangelist, discharge all the duties of your ministry" (4:5).

With fine effect these two sides of this holy teaching are also set over against each other in

Paul's letter to the Corinthians. On the one hand there is the touch of caution, "So, if you think you are standing firm, be careful that you don't fall" (1 Corinthians 10:12). But lest this should be too strong it is followed by the word of assurance, "God is faithful; he will not let you be tempted beyond what you can bear. But when you are tempted, he will also provide a way out so that you can stand up under it" (10:13). And then the balance is made complete by the final word of gentle warning, "Therefore, my dear friends, flee from idolatry" (10:14). There is no discouragement, but there is no presumption. The danger is real, but the security is ample; not, however, for blind, presuming rashness, but for watchful, humble, holy and persevering obedience.

The Master's Teaching

We find the same spirit of mingled warning and encouragement in all the teachings of the great Master. "My sheep," He says, "shall never perish; no one can snatch them out of my hand" (John 10:27-28). But just as truly does He also teach, "My sheep listen to my voice; I know them, and they follow me" (10:27). Again He exclaims, "You did not choose me, but I chose you and appointed you to go and bear fruit—fruit that will last" (15:16). Surely no promise could be stronger and no purpose more steadfast. Yet in this very connection we have the tender admonition, "Remain in me, and I will remain in you" (15:4). "If you obey my commands, you will remain in my love" (15:10). "If anyone does not remain in me, he is like a branch that is thrown away and withers; such branches are picked up, thrown into the fire and burned" (15:6).

In *Pilgrim's Progress*, when the pilgrims were introduced to the "Palace Beautiful," the interpreter showed them many beautiful pictures, some full of alluring loveliness and transporting hope, some full of dark and awful warning. On the one side were the visions of grace and glory, on the other the prisoner of despair in the iron cage, and the awful dream of the judgment day. And, as Christian came forth he said to his kind interpreter, "These things make me both hope and fear."

So God still teaches us. The Bible is no system of cast-iron dogmas. But as the wise, firm and gentle hand of a loving teacher and guide, it adjusts its messages to our situation and condition, whether of depression or false security. If we have an attitude of willful disobedience, it has no absolute promise of unconditional security, but words of stern and terrible awakening and warning. But for an attitude of humble trust and watchful obedience it has nothing but encouragement and the assurance of God's everlasting faithfulness and love.

It speaks to us, therefore, in many tones and from many standpoints, and is indeed "useful for teaching, rebuking, correcting and training in righteousness, so that the man of God may be thoroughly equipped for every good work" (2 Timothy 3:16-17).

A Place of Dependence

There is, then, real danger of declension, even on the part of a consecrated Christian, should he for one moment become separated from Christ, or relax his vigilance and constant dependence. Sanctification is not a state of infallible holiness, but a place of dependence upon Christ and abiding communion with Him. "No one who lives in him keeps on sinning" (1 John 3:6); but "apart from me you can do nothing" (John 15:6). And the strongest saint will, like Simon Peter, make the most desperate failure whenever he trusts his own strength, or attempts to stand alone.

Indeed, we are never truly safe till, like Peter, we have learned our constant danger and our need of Jesus every moment. Let us never forget that declension after consecration would be for us a fearful thing. The most terrific delusions of the world's history have usually originated with those who have had much light before. And failure, after all that the Lord has brought us into, would be unutterly sad and utterly disastrous.

Friend, let us abide in Him. Let us put on the whole armor of God that we may stand against the wiles of the devil. Let us adhere faithfully to His holy Word, and walk in obedience to all His commandments. And above all, let us depend implicitly upon His keeping, fearing to take one step alone. We need not fear while He holds our hand

and leads us safely in the most difficult paths, and makes us walk upon our high places.

The Causes of Failure

What were the causes of Israel's declension? The first of these seems to have been a superficial experience and knowledge of God. The language in which their declension is introduced implies that much of their piety arose from the influence of Joshua and the generation that had accompanied him. When he and they had passed from the stage, the nation returned to its deeper and truer spirit. Israel simply manifested the disposition that had been there before, but had been kept in check by the predominant influence of others.

There are many persons whose religious condition is a reflection of the influence of others, to a far greater extent than they dream. They are like young Joash, who served the Lord during all the days of his godly adopted father Jehoiada, but who immediately turned back to evil when he was gone. These people manifest much sympathetic goodness under the influence of favorite teachers, and in seasons of deep religious excitement they may even seem to pass through a real experience of spiritual life with its accompanying emotions and many of its fruits. But it is possible that much of this may be seated in the emotions, and may be the result of influence and feeling rather than radical conviction and transformation of character.

The test will come to such souls when these favorable influences are withdrawn, when they are no

longer pressed forward by stronger spirits and up-
held by helpful surroundings, but are met by opposition, misunderstanding, persecution and
uncongenial associations of every kind. Then it will
appear whether this purpose is rooted in God, and
their spirit truly united with a living Christ and
abiding in Him as the source and strength of life and
holiness. If this is so, they will continue, even amid
isolation and opposition, to stand steadfast to the
truth and will of God. Like Jeremiah's picture of the
man that trusts in the Lord, and whose help the
Lord is, they "will be like a tree planted by the
water that sends out its roots by the stream. It does
not fear when heat comes; its leaves are always
green. It has no worries in a year of drought and
never fails to bear fruit" (Jeremiah 17:8).

The Secret of Victory

The secret of Joshua's victory was that he had
long before learned to stand alone. When the
faithless spies and the whole congregation refused
to follow him and even threatened to destroy him,
with his solitary companion he stood steadfast to
God and principle. Therefore, when the multitude
afterwards followed, his purpose was not affected
by their favor or faithlessness, but he could look
them in the face and say, "Choose for yourselves
this day whom you will serve . . . But as for me
and my household, we will serve the LORD"
(Joshua 24:15).

This must be the secret of steadfastness in every
consecrated life. You must know the truth for

yourself and commit yourself to it even if you have to stand alone. You must be so persuaded of it that you cannot surrender it even if you die. And you must so know the Lord, for yourself and not for another, that even if all the Christians in the world should fail, you could still stand exclaiming, "Christ is true, and Christ is mine, and I know Him whom I have believed."

If you have thus learned Christ, the presence or the absence of people will not affect your life and testimony. Men may come and men may go, but you will go on forever. You will be able to say, like the heroic men of Babylon, "O Nebuchadnezzar, we do not need to defend ourselves before you in this matter. If we are thrown into the blazing furnace, the God we serve is able to save us from it, and he will rescue us from your hand, O king. But even if he does not, we want you to know, O king, that we will not serve your gods or worship the image of gold you have set up" (Daniel 3:16-17).

The second cause of Israel's declension was their failure to do thorough work, especially in separating from and exterminating their enemies. We read in the beginning of the book of Judges of many of the tribes of Canaan whom they should have thoroughly subjugated, that the children of Judah could not drive out the inhabitants of the valley (1:19). And that the children of Benjamin did not drive out the Jebusites that inhabited Jerusalem (1:21). Nor did Manasseh drive out the inhabitants of Beth Shan and her towns, but the

Canaanites would dwell in the land (1:27). Nor did Ephraim drive out the Canaanites in Gezer, but the Canaanites dwelt in Gezer among them. This was true of many of the other tribes as well. Not only were the foreign tribes allowed to live among them, but Israel, in some cases, put the Canaanites to tribute (1:28), making it even a profitable business and a source of income to have them remain. All this despite the fact that the Lord had commanded their utter extermination.

And still worse, we find them even entering into forbidden alliances with them, and also intermarrying among their sons and daughters (3:5-6). God's command to them had been, "When the LORD your God has delivered them over to you and you have defeated them, then you must destroy them totally. Make no treaty with them, and show them no mercy. Do not intermarry with them. Do not give your daughters to their sons or take their daughters for your sons" (Deuteronomy 7:2-3).

But in Judges we read, "The Israelites lived among the Canaanites, Hittites, Amorites, Perizzites, Hivites and Jebusites. They took their daughters in marriage and gave their own daughters to their sons, and served their gods" (Judges 3:5-6). Israel had become content with the victories that had subdued their more formidable foes and that had given them the chief strongholds of the land. But in a thousand little places the enemy still lurked and lingered and gradually became tolerated. The danger of their continuance did not seem very great, and the trouble and cost of their extermination was greater than the courage and patience of Israel. Thus they were suffered to remain, half conquered, and for the time, wholly subordinate. In a little while it became a source of profit to collect tribute from these bold giants, and so many of them were made tributary to Israel, contrary to the divine command.

A little later, relations of friendship and fellowship began to be established, and before long they were intermarrying with the tribes of Israel and raising a mongrel race in which the true seed would soon be wholly extinguished. And the worst of all, they naturally began to serve the idols of their heathen friends, and to mingle in all the abominations of their unholy religion. Thus they became in the end really apostate from the worship of the true God altogether.

This is the sad story of the development of evil in many lives that once seemed wholly consecrated. Little sins are left unsubdued. Like Saul, they destroy the Amalekites, but they spare Agag their king for some good purpose as they suppose, and keep the best of the spoil with the idea that they are going to sacrifice it unto the Lord. They have not the courage to deal bravely and firmly with evil. After a while they begin to turn it to profitable account, and tolerate certain forms of sin and worldliness because of advantage. Their business interests would be ruined by too rigid a conscientiousness, for some of their investments are not wholly separated from forbidden associations. The profits, at least, will be divided with the Lord, and the end will sanctify the means. A thousand specious and plausible excuses are made for things that ought to be thoroughly put aside, and which, like the Canaanites, they put under tribute and try to justify because of some advantage that can be brought out of them.

By and by, the social element is introduced. Families that were separated from unholy friendships and ungodly alliances become mixed with the world in the social reception, the promiscuous dance, or perhaps in the milder form of the church entertainment. The old people still retain their separation, yet they let their sons and daughters mingle with the Canaanites. They do not shrink from even permitting the marriage of a Christian girl with the godless man. Or perhaps they receive into their home, as the bride of their son, some bright and fascinating daughter of fashion who soon succeeds in subverting all the separation to God that has been left. Soon it is not far to the last step of the worship of idolatry, the unrestrained career of worldly amusement, covetousness and the carnival of godless selfishness and pleasure.

David Livingstone tells of a singular creature which he found in Africa, called the lion ant. It attacks and destroys the strongest victims by a master piece of strategy. Excavating a little pit in the dry sand, in the form of an inverted cone, running to a point at the bottom, it sits down at the base of its little pitfall and waits for some unsuspecting beetle or insect to tread too near the edge to this

strange excavation. In a moment the insect has lost
its balance and rolls down the side of the little pit
where the lion ant waits for its prey.

Not, however, directly and instantly does the
destroyer attack its victim. This might be too un-
equal a contest for the little strategist. But it suddenly opens its sharp little mouth, formed like a
pair of powerful scissors, and with one quick
movement cuts off a limb from the unsuspecting
victim, and then disappears out of sight. Slowly
the mutilated creature recovers itself and climbs
up the slippery side to the pit. But just as it
reaches the summit its footing slips again and it
tumbles once more into the jaws of the little mon-
ster. Another quick movement, and another limb
is gone. Again the wounded insect gathers up its
remaining strength and makes another ascent of
the side of this deathtrap, but the result is the
same as before. Again it sinks to receive a fresh
blow, and the process is repeated until at length it
is so dismembered that it has not strength enough
even to attempt to escape, but sinks, a bleeding,
suffering mass, into the hands of its enemy, who
devours at leisure the antagonist that it would not
have dared to approach directly.

This, alas, is the story of many a defeated and
ruined life. Some little adversary that was not
even dreaded has been the final destroyer, not
by one bold attack, but by a thousand little
wounds that at last have left the victim helpless
to resist or to return. Saul's career is a sad example of a noble beginning, ending in mournful

disaster. And the saddest part of it is the very smallness of the cause where the pathway of declension and ruin began. It was simply in this very thing of refusing to deal firmly with the enemies of God. The reason of his failure was because of his deeper fear to deal firmly with the sin and self-will of his own heart.

Saul's failure to slay Agag, and his soft dealings with the Amalekite chief, were but the outward type of his tolerance of a greater giant in his own heart. His own self-will and the spirit of disobedience which, Samuel told him, was expressed by his conduct in this case, were the grounds of his rejection and the secret of his final ruin. But now Saul did not go down all at once. For nearly 10 years he still sat upon Israel's throne and worked out the dreadful proceeds of sin's development. It led from step to step, until at last a branded murderer, a slave of blind and furious passion, and an awful instrument of Satan's very possession, he closed his wretched life in tragedy almost as dark as the story of Judas.

Oh! let us beware how we tolerate a single sin, how we leave an enemy in the land, how we make terms with any forbidden thing, how we enter into alliances with the world, or let its spirit touch our fondest affections. We cannot serve God and mammon. We cannot compromise with any evil thing and remain in the land of promise. We cannot abide in His love without keeping His commandments.

"Therefore come out from them
   and be separate,
      says the Lord.
Touch no unclean thing,
   and I will receive you."
"I will be a Father to you,
   and you will be my sons and daughters,
      says the Lord Almighty."
      (2 Corinthians 6:17-18)

CHAPTER 11

The Church's Inheritance

*Then Jesus came to them and said, "All author-
ity in heaven and on earth has been given to me.
Therefore go and make disciples of all nations,
baptizing them in the name of the Father and of
the Son and of the Holy Spirit, and teaching
them to obey everything I have commanded you.
And surely I am with you always, to the very
end of the age." (Matthew 28:18-20)*

The whole story of the book of Joshua may be
applied, in a broader sense, to the people of
God collectively, and especially to the New Testament Church. In an important sense the whole
body of Christians may be called the spiritual Israel. And the history of God's ancient people is
full of interesting parallels and lessons for us, even
if they may not be exact types in this respect.

The failure of Israel to enter into the land of
promise through unbelief had its parallel in the rejection of Christ by His own countrymen, and the
consequent rejection of the Jewish people from
the privileges of the gospel. But as for ancient Is-

rael there was still a period of probation and long-suffering. It lasted for 40 years, affording individuals the opportunity of entering into the spiritual blessings of God's covenant. Likewise, there intervened a similar period, after Christ's rejection by His own people, before the final destruction of Jerusalem and the dispersion of the Jews. And as there were some of even the first generation of Israel who believed, so there were exceptions in the ministry of Christ and His disciples from among even that unbelieving nation who gladly accepted their Messiah and entered into their spiritual inheritance.

The glorious career of Joshua—the crossing of the Jordan, the conquest of Canaan, and the dividing of the inheritance among the tribes of Israel—has a striking parallel in the New Testament. We can parallel the death and resurrection of Jesus, the descent of the Holy Spirit at Pentecost, and the triumphs of Christianity, when the Church, to a very great extent, claimed her inheritance of power, purity and blessing, and entered upon the conquest of the world for Christ, until there was scarcely a region of the globe where the gospel was not at least planted, and the strongholds of Satan challenged and shaken. The crossing of the Jordan may well illustrate the cross of Calvary and the experience of death and resurrection that was so emphasized in primitive Christianity. The new covenant has its counterpart in the coming of the Holy Spirit and the gospel of full and free salvation.

The death of Moses and the advent of Joshua, whose very name is suggestive of Jesus, suggest the transition which then actually came from the law to the gospel. The victories of Canaan had their counterpart in the triumphs of primitive Christianity. The dividing of the inheritance foreshadowed the various gifts of the Holy Spirit distributed to the church.

The supernatural element that runs through the entire story of the conquest of Palestine was more than realized in the first centuries of Christianity in the manifestations of the divine presence and power, in signs and wonders and mighty deeds. And the choice possessions, won by Caleb, Othniel, Acsah, and others, remind us of the transcendent examples of piety, faith, love, knowledge and holy power and usefulness which adorned the annals of the early Church.

The failure of Israel to enter promptly and fully into its whole inheritance also finds its counterpart in the Church of the New Testament. With all its fresh beauty and divine glory, still there was much of human imperfection and melancholy failure.

The old cry, "There are still very large areas of land to be taken over" (Joshua 13:1), "How long will you wait before you begin to take possession of the land that the LORD, the God of your fathers, has given you" (18:3), is echoed back in more than one of Paul's sorrowful admonitions to the churches he loved. It also appears still more strongly in the appeals and warnings of the Son of

God to the seven churches of Asia, through the last messages of the Holy Spirit, 60 years after His ascension. There we find Him saying to the strongest of these churches, "I hold this against you: You have forsaken your first love" (Revelation 2:4). To another He says, "You have a reputation of being alive, but you are dead. Wake up! Strengthen what remains and is about to die, for I have not found your deeds complete in the sight of my God" (3:1-2). And yet again, "You say, 'I am rich; I have acquired wealth and do not need a thing.' But you do not realize that you are wretched, pitiful, poor, blind and naked" (3:17).

Historical Parallels

Already, even in the lifetime of Paul and John, the primitive Church had allied itself sufficiently with the world to open the door for many of the errors that afterward entered and overwhelmed the purity of the early Church.

The fearful declension of ancient Israel, leading before long to the dark chapter of the book of Judges and their shameful compromise with the heathen world and subjugation to its power, is more than paralleled in the story of the dark ages of medieval Christianity through the same causes; namely, the failure of God's people to separate themselves from sin and worldliness and to enter into their full inheritance. The purity and strength of apostolic Christianity were speedily lost in the unspeakable corruptions of an apostate church. All the errors and abominations of that anti-Christian system took the place of the Church of God for 1,200 years. It has been well called a "baptized heathenism."

Many of the pictures of the book of Judges might find a vivid counterpart in the story of the middle ages. The graphic picture of Micah and his mother, with its strange intermingling of dishonesty, religion and ritualism, almost seems like a parable of much of the religious life of such a period, and, indeed, is not without its parallels in our own day. Like Micah's sanctuary, many a church has been built out of ill-gotten gains. And, like Micah himself, many a formalist has folded his arms in the midst of violence and sin and said, "Now I know that the LORD will be good to me, since this Levite has become my priest" (Judges 17:13).

Notwithstanding this there were many exceptions in ancient Israel—a wise and patriotic Deborah, a brave and faithful Barak, a divinely called Gideon, a single-hearted Jephthah, and a mighty Samson. And, so, even in the darkest ages of Christianity, there have not been wanting those who had not defiled their garments. There are many who, at times, dared to rise up for God against those that did wickedly, and shed a divine luster on their times and names. Such were the noble army of the martyrs and confessors—Waldo, Wycliffe, Huss, Savonarola, Bernard and Bede.

Israel's Reformation

At length the time of reformation came to ancient Israel, when Samuel, the prophet, arose to recall his people to their ancient faith and prepare them for the coming kingdom. Such a ministry in our own time was that of Luther and the Reformation, calling back the Church of God to her ancient faith, and arousing her to claim her lost inheritance. But Samuel's mighty work was in a measure ineffectual, and was followed for a time by the counterfeit kingdom of Saul and the false and worldly aims of his countrymen, that led them into a separation from God that left its effects for half a century. Likewise, the revived Christianity of the Reformation has not been perfect, and, like ancient Israel, the Church, delivered from her immediate foe, has given herself up to a great degree to a spirit of worldliness and to look for her kingdom in a forbidden world. There is much today of the spirit of Saul in nominal Christianity: the pride that finds its satisfaction in earthly gifts, talents and successes, and fails to recognize the true King, who, like the rejected David, waits for His throne as the "despised and rejected of men."

The Final Victory

The kingdom of David seems to prefigure the true triumphs of our coming King, and the ushering in of His dominion in the final victory of Christianity.

The peaceful and splendid throne of Solomon completes the picture of the millennial glory that is to be the consummation of the Christian age. Then will come the full inheritance of grace and glory, both for God's ancient people and the Church and the bride of the Lamb.

What, then, for us, in the Church of God today, is the teaching of this ancient book?

It summons her to her glorious crusade of conquest against the enemies of Christ. Never was there an age more full of encouragement for the good fight of faith and the conquest of the world for Christ. The whole land is set before us. Every avenue of influence at home, and every missionary field abroad, is open for the church's zeal and holy enterprise. The triumphs of the gospel in the past 50 years have not been unworthy of comparison with Pentecost, or even with Joshua's campaigns. True, it has been but a small section of the nominal church that has dared to claim these victories, but the recompense has been sufficient to call forth far higher achievements and aspirations.

Especially should the near prospect of the coming kingdom arouse us to go forth and win for our glorious Captain the crown of all the world, until every citadel of heathendom and every stronghold of sin will have become a monument of His grace and power.

More emphatically still, let the tender lesson of Rahab in the beginning, and the cities of refuge at the close, remind us that our supreme conflict is for the souls of sinful men. And beyond all the questions of dogmas, and the discussions of principles, and the undermining of systems of error and iniquity, let our objective point be individual men and women, and our highest and brightest trophies, the transformed lives of the most helpless and degraded of our race.

Let us, like Joshua and Israel, go in and possess all our inheritance. The Church has been slack to do this, and is still slack. She has not claimed her full inheritance of knowledge and truth, nor entered into all the fullness of God's precious promises.

She has not entered into her full inheritance of holiness, but has been content to look upon a life of sanctity and devotedness as an exceptional and occasional exhibition of individual temperament rather than as the duty and privilege of every child of God.

She has not entered into her full inheritance of faith, nor recognized the power that lies latent in taking God at His word and daring to claim all that He has spoken. A life of becoming faith and remarkable answers to prayer is regarded as something special and wonderful, a sort of peculiar calling on the part of some individual of exalted piety.

She has not entered into her full inheritance of love and unity, but has been rent with strifes, divisions, jealousies and controversies, which have left Hebron in the hands of the Anakim and her Lord wounded "at the house of [his] friends" (Zechariah 13:6).

And she has failed to enter into her full inheritance of supernatural power. The gifts of Pentecost have never been recalled, but have only been imperfectly claimed. Natural talent, human learning and worldly influence have been their weak and insufficient substitutes. Let us go in and possess all the land. All power is given unto our Joshua in heaven and in earth, and lo! He is with us always.

"For God did not give us a spirit of timidity, but a spirit of power, of love and of self-discipline" (2 Timothy 1:7). Let us, therefore, stir up the gift of God that is in us. Let Zion hear her Master crying, "Awake, awake, O Zion, clothe yourself with strength. Put on your garments of splendor" (Isaiah 52:1). "Arise, shine, for your light has come, and the glory of the LORD rises upon you" (60:1).

The almighty presence of our risen Lord is sufficient for any obedient service which we will dare to attempt in His strength and name. Let us put on the whole armor of the Lord. "Be strong in the Lord and in his mighty power" (Ephesians 6:10). Clothed in all the fullness of the unchanging Paraclete, let the Church of God go forth to the last campaign of the great conflict.

Let the Church remember the necessity of separation from sin and the world if she would overcome her enemies and possess her full inheritance. She must cross the Jordan and let its unbridged torrents roll between her and the world. She must know the true meaning of circumcision and let Gilgal roll away the reproach of Egypt from her spirit and person. She must watch against the sin of Achan, and not let the accursed thing touch her spotless hands. She must take no tribute from the Canaanites, nor lean upon the world in the slightest measure for her support.

She must separate from forbidden alliances with the ungodly, and stand "like the dawn, fair as the moon, bright as the sun, majestic as the stars in procession" (Song of Songs 6:10). The secret of her weakness and failure is that she has gone, like Israel, into a forbidden league with the tribes of the land. She has put her head, like Samson, in Delilah's lap, and her locks are shorn, and all her shaking of herself will not renew her strength until she has taken the place of the Nazirite and separated herself from a defiling and hostile world. "Come out of her, my people," is the Master's call. When the Church obeys it, she will stand forth in her primitive purity and power and draw all men unto her Lord.

CHAPTER 12

The Heavenly Canaan

*Instead, they were longing for a better coun-
try—a heavenly one. Therefore God is not
ashamed to be called their God, for he has prepared a city for them. (Hebrews 11:16)*

Christian hope has always loved to link the
land of promise with our heavenly inheritance. The sacred poetry of the past is full of this
sweet and sacred imagery. Jordan is the swelling
flood of death, and the sweet fields beyond are the
images of that heavenly land.

Where everlasting spring abides,
    And never withering flowers,
And death, the narrow stream, divides
    That heavenly land from ours.

The vital objection to the logic of this theory is
that heaven essentially differs from the earthly
Canaan in most of the features that chiefly distin-
guished the latter. Canaan was a land of conflict
and hard-won victory, while heaven will have no
foes to overcome, and all its crowns will be those

of accomplished triumph and peaceful recompense. Heaven will have no Jericho, no Gibeon, no valley of Achor, no failure such as that of Achan, and no sad declension such as that which followed Israel's entry into Canaan. And yet there are some points in which the misinterpretation is not without its lessons. Canaan was Israel's home, their place of rest after the conflicts in the wilderness, and the realization of long-deferred hopes and promises.

And so there remains a rest for the people of God on the heaven side of the grave where they will be at home. It is a place where "they will rest from their labor, for their deeds will follow them" (Revelation 14:13). It is a place where the long deferred hopes and expectations of life will be realized at length, and all their wanderings and trials will forever cease. God forbid that we should abate anything of the blessed meaning of heaven, where all the ransomed wait in unspeakable felicity for the greater inheritance that lies still farther beyond.

It is of this better inheritance that the ancient Canaan was really the type; for there is a better inheritance even than heaven. Christian hope is always connected in the New Testament Scriptures, not with death and the state of the departed, but with the second coming of the Lord Jesus and the millennial glory that is then to be ushered in. Even the earthly Canaan itself was but the transient home of the seed of Abraham. It looked forward both in type and promise to a future age when Israel should inherit their full patrimony, and when all the children of faith should possess, through the age of glory, their land of promise.

Like the ancient Canaan, it is to be introduced by the true Joshua, the Lord Jesus Christ. There is no millennium promised in the Scriptures apart from His personal coming. The heavens have received Him, according to the language of the apostles, "until the time comes for God to restore everything" (Acts 3:21). But He is coming again, and His appearing and His kingdom will be simultaneous.

The Hope of His Appearing

Like the ancient Canaan, only the children of faith and obedience will possess this inheritance. Perhaps many of the ancient Israel were saved who never entered the land of promise. And so it is possible to belong to the people of God and yet lose much of the glory and recompense connected with the hope of His appearing. "He will appear a second time, not to bear sin, but to bring salvation to those who are waiting for him" (Hebrews 9:28). "With him will be his called, chosen and faithful followers" (Revelation 17:14).

The millennium, like Canaan, must be conquered, too. Not without resistance will He enter upon His kingdom. The world's greatest conflict will just precede its millennial Sabbath. The mighty Captain of the millennial armies sits upon a white horse with garments dyed in blood. The name King of Kings appears on His vesture and upon His thigh. He will come forth as a mighty conqueror, treading under His feet the hosts of Antichrist and the powers of hell, and scattering His enemies, as the feet of Nebuchadnezzar's image, like the chaff of the summer threshing floors. "For he must reign until he has put all his enemies under his feet" (1 Corinthians 15:25). The battles of Joshua and the conquests of David are the living types of the advent struggles and the Armageddon war.

The Lord's coming will bring not only conflict, but victory. Joshua's campaign was an uninterrupted and complete triumph until it was finished. There was no king in all the Hittite confederacy that had not been overthrown. And so our Lord is to put down all authority and opposition and reign without a rival over the millennial earth. The day is surely coming when every evil thing that lifts its head in proud defiance will be laid prostrate at His feet. Not forever will right be on the scaffold and wrong upon the throne. He will "bring about justice for his chosen ones" (Luke 18:7).

Error at length will cease to deludes, selfishness to prey on holiness; and injustice, vice and crime will no longer defile and destroy the creation of God. The hour is coming when the adversaries of the Church and of the soul will be remembered only as a vanished dream. We will seek for them but they will not be found. The proud empires of the world, the blasphemous and defiant power of Antichrist, and even Satan himself, will be cast out from God's fair inheritance, and the kingdom will be given to the saints of God and the Prince of Peace.

The conquests of Canaan were not a truce with the adversary, not an attempt to transform their adversaries into peaceful friends, but their utter extinction. And so the coming of the Lord is to involve the destruction of His enemies. The gospel age is the time for evangelization and the day for the world's peaceful submission and conversion. But when the Master comes He will "overthrow with the breath of his mouth and destroy by the splendor of his coming" (2 Thessalonians 2:8), everything that exalted itself against the obedience of Christ.

Our Inheritance

His coming will bring to us our inheritance. Then will Abraham and David possess the literal fullness of their ancient covenants, and the land on which their feet rested for a time will be their own and the home of their offspring. Then will the disciples who followed Jesus in His days of rejection, sit on 12 thrones judging the tribes of Israel. Then will we possess our complete redemption, spirit, soul and body, perfectly restored to the image of God, and our lost dominion over the earth will be given back through our exalted Head. Then will the saints of God receive the recompenses of their lives of service and suffering, and those who have overcome will wear the crowns of victory and glory which He has promised to the faithful and triumphant. Then will each soul find its perfect sphere and enter upon the service for which its earthly training has qualified it. And doubtless there will be a Hebron of exalted fellowship and love for every brave Caleb; a Kiriah Sepher of boundless knowledge for every conquering Othniel; a fountain of life, with its upper and nether springs, for every true Acsah who has dared to claim her full inheritance; a double inheritance for every true Ephraimite that has dared to conquer it in the days of earthly battle; a city of honor and service for every Levite who has been true to his consecration; and a Timnath Serah of everlasting light and glory for every faithful Joshua.

Our full inheritance is yet to come. All we know of Jesus in His indwelling fullness and victorious life is but the type of the glory that awaits us at His advent. All we know of truth here is "a poor reflection as in a mirror; . . . then I shall know fully, even as I am fully known" (1 Corinthians 13:12).

All we know of holiness here is but a shadow of that hour when we will be like Him, as we see Him as He is. All we know of physical redemption is but a prophetic foretaste of the glorious life that will thrill every frame with the resurrection joy. All we know of service for the Master is but the blundering attempt of the school boy as he learns the mere alphabet of knowledge, compared with the mighty faith and divine power with which we will be workers together with Him in the transformation of the millennial earth at the inauguration of His glorious kingdom.

He is educating us to bear a far more exceeding, even an eternal weight of glory. Let us be apt learners, and by and by we will look back with amazement to our earthly childhood and scarcely recognize the trembling and blundering beginner who once struggled and toiled through the years of time, and claimed the inheritance that was to be so much more vast and transcendent than his brightest earthly dream.

And best of all, He will be Himself our Eternal inheritance. "Now the dwelling of God is with men, and he will live with them. They will be his people, and God himself will be with them and be their God" (Revelation 21:3).

The Heavenly Canaan

Hallelujah! hark, the sound,
   From the center to the skies,
Wakes above, beneath, around,
   All creation's harmonies.

He shall reign from pole to pole,
   With illimitable sway;
He shall reign when, like a scroll,
   Yonder heavens have passed away.

Then the end—beneath His rod
   Man's last enemy shall fall.
Hallelujah! Christ in God,
   God in Christ is all in all.

SCRIPTURE INDEX

191